ATTENTION READERS! The original *Never Out of Season* is now ten years old. The world has changed considerably. Although my viewpoints on the challenges of managing our finances have changed less, it is time for me to comment on and criticize many of my original thoughts. Rather than burden you readers with a whole new book, we have reprinted the original (with updated charts and graphs) and inserted an addendum to each chapter giving my current perceptions of the subject. Hopefully, what I believe I have learned will be helpful to you. I am sure you will agree with me that I haven't learned enough to write a whole new book.

Never Out of Season

A Timeless Guide
to Building Your Wealth

DAVID W. HUNTER

LOOKOUT FARM PUBLICATIONS

Pittsburgh

ISBN 0-8191-8549-3

Grateful acknowledgment is made of the following for permission
to reprint previously published material:

Johnson' Charts, Inc.: Selected charts and graphs from the 1991
Johnson's Charts. Reprinted by permission of Johnson's Charts, Inc.

Salomon Bros.: Chart titled "The Asset Derby" from *Stocks Are Hot—
Collectibles Are Not*. Reprinted by permission of Salomon Bros.

Printed in Canada.

Printed on acid-free paper.

3   5   7   9   10   8   6   4   2

To Pete, Sue, and Crock,
With the hope that they can build
on this foundation.

Contents

Ah, when to the heart of man

    Was it ever less than a treason

To go with the drift of things,

    To yield with a grace to reason,

And bow and accept the end

    Of a love or a season?

from *Reluctance*, by Robert Frost

Acknowledgments

WRITING THIS BOOK TOOK A CHUNK OF MY SPARE TIME FOR almost two years. That is a good bit longer than I originally expected, since I knew about what I wanted to say and have given many one-hour talks with only ten minutes of preparation. But, I have a full-time job and several *"part-time"* jobs that keep me busy. The book would not be done, however, without the assistance of Marisa (MJ) Fera, who joined me a couple of years ago to develop and coordinate this book project, among other responsibilities. MJ, in her position as my associate, was instrumental throughout the project, demanding that I make the text and its concepts clear to her before they were included in the book, assisting in the research (especially all the charts and graphs you will be using), and the editing of the many drafts. Our primary aim in this book is to present those investing concepts in such a fashion that any *kid* of whatever age or financial status can understand them. Therefore, if you, the reader, understand what I am saying in this opus, you can thank MJ. I am grateful to her for all the time and effort she put into this book—and for putting up with me.

This book would not have gotten done so quickly without the help and patience of Sue Haberlein. Sue did barrels of word processing, but her real contribution was in taking care of all the other people in my full-time and part-time jobs—the vast majority of my clients and friends would rather talk with Sue than with me, a fact that surprises no one who knows me. Therefore, if you, the reader, enjoy this opus, you can thank Sue. I am grateful to her for her efforts—and for putting up with MJ and me.

Three other people also deserve individual thanks. Jim Frost edited the final drafts of the book over the last few months and knows what he is doing in the world of letters. Dennis Ciccone knows what he is doing in the world of books and was most helpful in getting this published. Chip Burke, a schoolteacher, came into my office to work part-time for two months and ended up having to read and comment on several chapters of the book. He also worked very hard on a mathematical equation, which we subsequently abandoned. Chip knows what he is doing in the world of baseball.

Aside from the individuals mentioned, there are whole groups of people to thank. My clients, for example, who are also my friends, have been very understanding. The time taken to write this book might otherwise have been used to solve some of their financial problems. On the other hand, if the book is helpful to them in understanding how I approach their problems, perhaps this trade-off will come out even in the long run. The people in my firm were also most understanding of the fact that I was fussing with this book, and were nice enough to let me go ahead and do it. My family deserves even more credit, since writing the book took a good bit of time away from fixing the fences on the farm, a job marginally within my capabilities. Next year I will fix more fences.

Finally, I should probably even acknowledge the contribution of those who would normally play golf against me—it probably cost them some money. Those who would have been golf partners of mine should thank me for writing the book—it probably saved them some money.

·

Acknowledgments in 2001...

I'll finish the second edition of *Never Out of Season* with the embarrassing confession that I have again used a chunk of my spare time over a year and a half simply to update the original issue of this glorified pamphlet. The older I get the more help I need, but the more help I get. My assistants have been wonderful.

First and foremost, I've had the joy of getting to know and working with Lauren Purnell, a.k.a. L.P., who, having finished high school in the summer of 1999, joined me for afternoon discussion and recording periods. She was great. When we started she knew nothing about finance or investing, but not only provided the ability to record my drivelings, but to question them and make sure she understood what I was saying before it became an acceptable addition to this effort. Because I was so slow, she had to come back again in the summer of '00 to get me through this. Her presence and help made what would have been drudgery into a very pleasurable experience. L.P. is now a sophomore at the University of Virginia, but if she'll come back again, we'll write something else.

Our very small firm is my dream home. Our clients are individuals and families who make my work a very pleasant experience. When we first started the firm about nine years ago, Penguin Books published an unsuccessful paperback edition of *Never Out of Season*. Three of my associates helped produce that bomb. Barbara Jene ("Surf") and Susan Conway have both moved on to what I expect are better jobs with higher pay, but Win Smathers, who worked diligently on the exhibits and charts, is still with our firm and part of our five-person team within the firm. To my knowledge, he deserves none of the blame for the lack of success of the paperback, but he has spilled a good bit of coffee on our rugs in the last few years. He blames me, I blame him, and everybody else blames both of us.

Sue Haberlein has been with me and suffered through all three editions. Sue's most time consuming task is usually that of the literary clean-up hitter who retyped all the scratches and notes that were given to her with a label of "finished draft." The fourth member of our team was fortunate enough to escape most of the book writing by joining us this past summer. Katie Kartsonas has two children with whom she spends part time, but becomes an associate two days a week to help me with security analysis. Chapter 14, the one on common stocks, was Katie's training course here at the firm. She passed the course easily and has been just as easily accepted by the whole firm.

The fifth member of our team is Jennifer Hughes, who didn't do any work on the book. What Jen has done is all the work while we're fussing with the book or some other unworthy project. I'll take that back. Jen collects money from and sends books to those victims across the country who send money in exchange for books. This is not an all consuming task.

My friend Barbara Lovejoy, a consultant to several companies who seems to spend a great deal of her time flying across the country, was kind enough to take the original book and a few draft chapters on her trips. I think she sleeps better on planes as a product of having the book with her, but her waking insights were most helpful.

Our publishing expert is Dennis Ciccone, whom we originally described as proficient in the world of books. Despite his many other activities, Dennis is still proficient in the world of books, guiding us through this process. He also found us an intelligent literary individual to read and clean up what we thought was a finished product. This time it was a delightful lady named Sona Vogel in New York City who managed to cover my grammatical deficiencies in an efficient and friendly manner.

In my view, virtually all of these people who have helped me range from young to very young. As a cranky old man, I preach about the decline and fall of American culture in the coming generation. These friends all force me to smile and admit the next generation would be wonderful if we could simply produce a few more like them.

A *Kid's* Book of Investment Policy

THE AIM OF THIS BOOK IS TO HELP YOU BETTER INVEST YOUR savings. Frankly, it will also save me time by providing my clients/ friends with an understanding of how I approach their investment problems. About 30 years ago, I wrote a pamphlet titled "An Intro- duction to Investment Policy" so the Wharton School of Business would give me a certificate of merit and let me stay in class. The certificate was quickly lost, but the policy pamphlet was not. I inflicted it on potential and new clients for a few years. When I gave them the pamphlet, I found I did not have to talk so much, and they did not have to listen to me so much, a happy circum- stance for both sides. After 30 years, I am trying again in a bit more detail, but I find, somewhat to my surprise, my basic approach has changed very little. Although I am in the autumn of my life (early autumn, of course!), I believe what someone once said: "Money is something that is never out of season."

As an individual, you are unique. Therefore, a good investment policy requires that you think about your particular situation. It requires that you establish your own practical goals by relating your financial situation and your aims to the investment world in a specific manner for a specific fit. This book presents various con- cepts and challenges to investing your savings well. What I want you to think about as you go through the book is how *you* fit the concepts I describe. If you are willing to take the time to make notes of your thoughts and reactions as you read this book, you will be well on your way to adopting and implementing your unique investment policy, a policy that will always be in season.

There are several concepts in this book which I strongly endorse and which are contrary to prevailing thought. These debatable ideas include:

1. No one can forecast the short-term stock market, but you can use the market fluctuations to your advantage.
2. A good investment policy comes from relating the individual to the investment world, not from using the investment world to dictate how each individual should be investing.
3. You should divide your portfolio of financial assets into groups based upon risk to principal.
4. The allocation of your financial assets to various types of investments should be consistent, varied only occasionally by the circumstances of your personal life but not by fluctuations in the markets.
5. You should keep your lendings conservative and short term, and take your risks with your ownership investments.
6. This business of investing is not an exact science, and you do not need mathematically precise approaches, fancy charts and graphs, or high-tech computer programs to be successful in the long term. The math necessary to be a successful investor does not exceed the eighth-grade level.
7. Successful investing requires neither vast knowledge nor secret or fancy techniques to quick riches; rather, over time, a simple but unique investment approach utilizing stocks and bonds will help you attain reasonable goals.

You have probably bought books or toys for children that were labeled "for ages 4 to 7" or "ages 8 to 10." This book is for *kids* of all ages, for that childlike wonder, that openness to new ideas, enables us to shake off rigid ideas of investment orthodoxy and also to look inside ourselves. One of my theories is that we never really grow up. It is generally accepted that kids should have a lot of fun. I think older kids should also have a lot of fun. For me, and I hope for you, this business of investing is simply a complex extension of the games we played as children, although it is certainly more rewarding financially. Over a period of time, investing even beats playing shortstop for the Pittsburgh Pirates, which would have been my first choice as a career, at least for half my life. Good investors are always open to new ideas, and I encourage you to come up with different ideas to make your investing journey. The approach I have set forth is certainly not immutable. Although it has been worthwhile for me and many of my clients/friends, I still regard other approaches as worthwhile—especially if they work for you. Differing viewpoints provide much of the fun, so I welcome yours.

This book does not try to be sophisticated; rather, it tries to be understandable, because it is most important that you grasp its ideas and shape them to suit yourself. It will show you how to survey the economic landscape and your own backyard. *You* can analyze your *individual* needs. It will show you how to set realistic personal goals and to measure how far you have to go. It will show you ways to get there and how to plan your route. You will be able to structure a portfolio that meets your needs and goals, and manage your portfolio according to this *personal* design *first* and market conditions second. But, most of all, it will help you build the vehicle that will carry you there through all seasons—*your unique investment policy.* Okay, kids, let's get started!

•

Wait a Minute...

It has been approximately ten years since I first started writing *Never Out of Season*. It's now mid-1999 as I begin critiquing my own work with the copy you're holding. I'll probably finish in the next century. The book is different in that it now has an additional, fortunately briefer, section immediately following each of the original chapters. This is my critique. I don't want to write a whole book on how wrong I was ten years ago. You might be surprised how little I've learned. I was.

I had several incentives for writing the original *Never Out of Season* and among the most prominent were the following:

1. New clients come in to see me, generally referred by a mutual friend and hopeful for some quick words of wisdom from me, which they never receive. From my standpoint, I want to use our time together to learn about the new client and not repetitively lecture on building an investment policy. I give them a book and use our session to learn about them rather than have the poor soul leave our first session without feeling both mentally and physically empty.
2. I have used my own urchins as targets, wanting them to get some feel for what I think I know about this investing business.
3. By 1989 I had largely developed an approach toward the investing challenges facing individuals that was simple enough so that kids could learn it by reading about it instead of listening to me. A highly regarded investment manager named Charlie Ellis wrote a wonderful book on investment policy for institutions. I'll flatter myself by saying I've used a somewhat parallel approach in my efforts for individuals.

One of my ambitions for the original edition was to have it used as a textbook in either a college class or perhaps an advanced high school class. Presumably the class would read the book and then spend several class sessions telling me where I was wrong. Years ago, I spent considerable time traveling around predominately western Pennsylvania colleges, talking to students about the subjects in this book. As it happened, strangely enough, my ambition was never realized; just as I finished the book, the colleges stopped inviting me. A major incentive for this second edition stems from my own stubbornness—if nobody else will critique my book, I'll do it myself.

Oddly enough, we have "sold" something over 40,000 copies of the original book. I put the word "sold" in quotes because I have probably managed to get some money for about 30,000 copies and managed to give away perhaps 10,000 copies to virtually anyone who would take one. Of the 40,000 copies distributed, I suspect that perhaps 5,000 have actually been read. Of those, at least eight to ten people have told me they really enjoyed it.

Thanks to my wonderful friend Ben Edwards, the firm of A. G. Edwards has been the biggest customer for the book. Ben liked it and decided that everyone else in the firm should read it. They don't read it, but he thought they should. When Ben decided to buy in bulk, he called me for our normal first tee negotiations. The question was book price instead of golf strokes. The conversation went roughly as follows:

Ben: "What's the price if I buy the book in lots of 1,000 or 1,500?"

Dave: "Well, the price on the inside cover is $16.95."

Ben: "Yeah, I saw that, but of course it's ridiculous."

Dave: "Yeah, I guess so. It certainly would be to you."

Ben: "Nobody in his right mind would pay that much for your book."

Dave: "How about $8?"

We ended up at six bucks per pop, apparently the appropriate price since we both left the conversation with the happy conclusion that we had ripped the other guy off.

I totally missed my target markets for the original edition. My hope had been that a few old "kids" would buy the book to check their investment policies and quite a few younger "kids" would read it if they were given the book. Well, the older "kids" were too smart to pay $16.95 for the book, and the younger "kids" either can't read or are too busy making millions in the stock market by ignoring my advice. As it turns out, stockbrokers read the book. They are supposed to know more than is in the book, but they are the ones who read the book, and perhaps they talk a few of their clients into skimming it.

When the original edition was released in 1992, I had some momentary fun pretending I was a real author. I made a few public appearances in support of book sales. One of these was a "Meet the Author" appearance at Borders Book Store on a cold and miserable winter Sunday afternoon. I dressed in my tweediest and sat in a soft chair in front of a fake fireplace and talked to the 30 or 40 people who appeared. They were of all descriptions and all ages, and I wondered what they had in common. I figured the session would take about 20 minutes and I would be out of there, but two hours later I was still fielding questions and answers. It finally dawned on me what this widely diverse group of people had in common: nothing to do on a Sunday afternoon.

Probably my biggest event was appearing on Pat Robertson's TV show, *The 700 Club*. Pat and I had two somewhat simultaneous conversations. The first was when we were on the air and Pat pretended he didn't know much about investing and was delighted to let the public know that my book was certainly a simple and easy contribution toward substantial investment knowledge. When we were off the air and they were either showing ads or singing, Pat and I had a second conversation in which I pretended I knew as much about investing as he did, which I didn't. I suspect neither of us pretended too well, since only three or four people across the nation ordered books at full retail price plus shipping charges. That appearance ended my promotional tour.

Someone pointed out as we were publishing the original edition that I should get some quotations from prominent friends in the investment business for the back cover, so I asked half a dozen industry friends to give me their thoughts with full poetic license. None of the comments were very complimentary, so my book consultants complained. I went back to my friends and asked for something nice. That took awhile. For this edition we're using the more accurate originals.

CHAPTER 1

The World in Which We Live

IN FORMULATING YOUR INVESTMENT POLICY, I HAVE FOUND that it is very important to relate your situation as an investor to the world in which you live. Therefore, understanding yourself financially as an individual or a family is only half the battle. If you are going to invest successfully over a period of time, you must have some awareness of this world to which you devote your savings. Further, it would please me if I leave you with the impression that we Americans are pretty lucky, that we investors are pretty important, and that we old kids are leaving you young kids some pretty formidable challenges.

In discussing investment policy with college students, for many years I usually started by defining money, inflation, and the various investment alternatives. Belatedly, however, I began to realize that most Americans—and my students in particular—had no clear understanding of America the Beautiful, of democracy and capitalism. We are free people, we are allowed to get rich, that much was understood. What was less clear was how the philosophical underpinnings of our nation give rise to that freedom and the opportunity for a superb standard of living. I gradually learned from the students that we had not all taken the same political science and economics courses, assuming we had taken any. Some of us had only taken a course titled Civics, from which we learned how the government is supposed to work (but certainly not how it does work). Practical economics courses are still largely nonexistent, at least those that pertain to our private enterprise system and how we ourselves relate to it. Yet, it is our political and economic world within which we develop our policy to invest and in which we ultimately invest our savings.

Each nation must have both a political system and an economic system. The function of a political system is to establish a government that passes rules and regulations allowing us to live together, it is hoped, in peace ("domestic tranquility") and for the betterment of all. Remember the Preamble to the Constitution? The function of an economic system is to provide as many goods and services as possible for the people.

We Americans all could profit from being more aware of our political system, so I'll spend a moment on it. We live in a democracy and elect our leaders through the vote of the people, a system that places the political power in the hands of the people (at least at election time). Perhaps more important, democracy implies the freedom of individuals to express themselves, both politically and economically, and certainly vocally. James Yard, one of the founders of the National Conference of Christians and Jews, expressed his thoughts on democracy as follows:

> Democracy is more than theory, it is not even a constitution or set of laws, democracy is the way you treat people—all people. It is a deep conviction of the value of personality and the eternal worth of the individual. Democracy cares about the everlasting rights of persons.

I like that. It tells me I am free, I am allowed to be opinionated, noisy, and do what I like as long as I do not hurt other people. In nondemocratic societies, the individual is not regarded highly enough to be considered as someone who can select those who govern. It is because we have such power as people that we have such rights as individuals. Remember the Bill of Rights?

Our economic system, called capitalism or the private enterprise system, is not well understood by most of us. The essence of private enterprise is the right of the individual to acquire assets, to be an owner, and even to become wealthy if that is one's good fortune. It is worth remembering that our democratically inspired Declaration of Independence did not promise happiness; it promised only the "pursuit of happiness." If we had a Declaration of Private Enterprise, it would not promise wealth; it would promise only the pursuit of wealth. We own our productive enterprises directly as individual shareholders or indirectly through pension plans, profit-sharing plans, or other institutions. We benefit as individuals, once again directly or indirectly, from the profits of these enterprises. We are allowed to be happy and to become wealthy.

From a philosophical standpoint, our economic system is far more fragile than our political system. We Americans almost unanimously endorse democracy. Even today, however, we debate our economic system. The alternative to our private enterprise system is clear: a collectivist economic system, such as socialism or communism, in which the government either owns our productive enterprises or dictates how such enterprises will operate and how the goods, services, and wealth will be distributed. The philosophy of a collectivist society is that the goods and services produced should be equitably distributed among the people, not on the basis of their contribution for producing them, but on the basis that each person should receive the same reward or result. Most of us capitalists endorse a system that provides equal opportunity for all but certainly rejects the concept of equal results. In other words, we want to be paid for our *efforts*, not simply receive the same pay as everybody else despite our efforts. Many of us may regret the fact that we have not achieved equal opportunity, but we do not see mandated equal results as a solution. Don't confuse democracy (one vote per person) with economics. In our view, the right of each individual to become economically successful itself makes a contribution to others by encouraging the successful person to invest capital in businesses that create new jobs as well as new or better products and services.

In periods when our economic system is performing poorly, for example during the Great Depression of the 1930s, political

3

advocates for changing the system pop up all across the country. If you are in San Francisco sometime (which you should be), visit Coit Tower, a picturesque tourist monument built as a make-work project during the pits of the depression. The murals inside Coit Tower, painted by unemployed artists, depict the worker as a husky, friendly hero and the businessman as a dour, unattractive character. Substantial numbers of Americans during that difficult period were very unhappy with American corporations, their managers, and even their shareholders. In such periods, the concept of socialism, having the government instead of individuals own our corporations, appeals to a substantial number of American voters.

Collectivism is still not dead, even as communism crumbles. Recently, Socialist International, a group representing 91 socialist political parties from around the world, met in New York City (at the Waldorf Astoria, of course). If you are as pleased as I am with the private enterprise system, it is worth bearing in mind that it can be changed to a collectivist system almost overnight at the ballot box. Even when our economy is doing wonderfully there is no total agreement that the private enterprise system should be maintained. When was the last time you saw a movie in which the businessman was portrayed as the hero?

A lack of cohesiveness in our national economic system can be traced partially to our educational system. What did you learn in high school about how our economic system works, how to get a job, why you should save, or how you should invest your money? Chances are the answer is zero. Perhaps this is one reason our savings rate is so low. When I was in college, these questions were not explicitly addressed. If there was an underlying philosophical debate in my college days, it centered on our economic system and whether we should have a collectivist or a private enterprise economy. I remember clearly a course taught by Professor Colston Warne, who, by coincidence, was the founder of Consumers Union, which produces *Consumer Reports*. Professor Warne taught the course by acting as an advocate for each economic system ranging from fascism to communism. Our American private enterprise system was somewhere in the middle. Good course, but none of us left it with the conviction that we Americans had something unique and worth preserving. Philosophically, private enterprise is attacked because it is based on *greed.* It is also not very intellectually appealing.

The compelling case for private enterprise is that it works. Certainly, if you look at the goods and services produced by the United States, Japan, or West Germany, there is not much debate as to whether the private enterprise system works. What makes the system work? If we substitute the word *incentive* for *greed,* maybe we will find the key. What makes us get up in the morning and go to work? As an investor, what leads you to make a particular investment? Incentive. Whether we are working or investing, we have the incentive to win economically. We have the incentive to work hard, to think, to achieve, and to get paid for it. This is why you are important as an investor. You are providing the capital to an enterprise with the incentive of a good return to yourself, but, at the same time, you are providing the capital and the incentive to someone else to work for themselves and for you. Why does the collectivist economy not work? If you are going to receive the same goods and services or compensation as the guy next to you, who is doing nothing, why should you work so hard?

A couple of years ago, some Red Chinese steel managers visited Pittsburgh, presumably on a mission to learn something about how to produce more steel. Their steel company required 200,000 workers to produce as much steel as U. S. Steel does with 25,000 workers. I was invited to spend an hour with them and through an interpreter tried to answer their questions. If I had any response that surprised them, it was simply my recommendation that they figure out some way to give their workers an incentive to work. The thought that an individual might want some incremental reward for doing useful work appeared to be a new concept to them.

What is occurring in our political and economic systems is important to you and your standard of living, particularly if you are young enough to see the resolution of these historic conflicts. Capitalism is clearly winning the philosophical debate. In 1990, a

headline appeared in the world-renowned *Pittsburgh Post-Gazette*—
"Russia Turns to Capitalism." I never thought I would live long
enough to witness the conclusion of the debate between the private
enterprise system and the collectivist societies. Think of all those
nations in the world that have been economically successful in the
past 20 years—the United States, West Germany Japan, etc.—and
they are invariably capitalistic nations. Now think of those nations
that have been unsuccessful economically over the past 20 years—
the USSR, the Russian satellites, China, etc.—and they invariably
have collectivist economies. We have witnessed in Europe the capit-
ulation of the collectivist economic societies and the recognition
that the private enterprise system, with its private ownership and
greed/incentives, is vastly superior in producing goods and services
for people.

One aspect of our political and economic machinations not
commonly discussed might be helpful to you in thinking about
your investment policy. Not all of us capitalists with strong opinions
and similar backgrounds on political and economic matters are, by
any means, in identical philosophical camps. One of the contrasts
I discovered in my brief political endeavors was that some of us
who did, in fact, take the same courses in school ended up with
different viewpoints on what is best for the nation. An interesting
contrast is between those like myself, who can be characterized as
people's capitalists, versus what I will refer to as *corporate capitalists*.
On matters such as tax policy, the people's capitalist is generally
advocating lower capital gains rates and/or supportive measures
benefiting the individual investor, small companies, and risk-
taking investments. The corporate capitalist is generally supportive of policies—tax policies in particular—that permit lower tax
rates or faster depreciation, both of which have substantial impact
on major companies.

In 1977, I had the privilege of breakfasting with Mike Blumenthal,
who as Secretary of the Treasury had joined the Carter administration from the Bendix Corporation. What we agreed on was that
the economy was in the pits and government tax policy changes

were necessary not only to balance the budget but also to get the economy off its duff. His approach was very clear: Give corporations incentives for making capital investments, such as rapid and liberal depreciation schedules, and thereby reduce the governmental burden on corporate America. However, we were miles apart on how to solve the problems, for I strongly advocated a reduced capital gains tax and those measures that would stimulate individual American investors to begin to take risks with their savings. Now that Mr. Blumenthal has left both the government and Unisys and the economy is sagging, I suspect we could have the same breakfast and express the same disagreements. What we would agree on is our basic belief in the private enterprise system and that Congress is inept.

As a people's capitalist, it is not my contention that the profitability of major corporations is unimportant, for it certainly is, and it is far more important than most Americans believe. It is my contention, however, that when savings are channeled into smaller, faster-growing companies, we are more closely contributing to those factors most important to an economy: new products, new services, and more jobs. As you watch the debates in Washington, D.C., on spending and tax proposals, ask yourself which way the currents are moving and how they might affect your investment patterns.

People's capitalism will be the approach of the future, simply because we live in a democratic system and must have a large percentage of our voting populace understand, believe in, and endorse our economic system. Otherwise, the people will simply use the ballot box to change the whole system. I am an optimist as to how Americans respond when they understand what is going on. The problem is we are living in an increasingly complex society and understanding what is going on requires a consistently higher level of education.

The winning of the old philosophical debates brings all of us American kids, once again particularly you younger kids, a new set of challenges with enormous implications for both our investments and our future standard of living. Chief among these challenges is the fact that we Americans are for the first time faced with international economic competition as we move toward an economic *one world*. We certainly have some strong, competitive advantages. We have lived with a system of competition since our founding, and we have strong natural resources, great schools, advanced technologies, and a strong infrastructure, to list a few. We have also developed some competitive disadvantages. Without debating the pros and cons of these, I will mention a few. First, our government and our businesses have developed an adversarial position. Instead of unity, we have conflict between our political and our economic systems, which must compete against nations where government and business are working toward the same goals. Second, our system of justice, assuming we still have a system of justice and not just a judicial system, has become a competitive disadvantage. It is amazingly slothful, expensive, and capable of making terrible decisions. No matter how you view these debates, our government and our litigious society have added serious new increments in the cost structures of our businesses, making it more difficult for us to compete internationally. The goods and services produced by our economic system depend on our savings and the investment of these savings in productive enterprises (that is the importance of you, the investor). As I see the future competition, it will be based to a great extent on knowledge and effort, and I ask myself whether our school systems and families are adequately developing our young people to meet these challenges. These are tough questions for Americans, who have enjoyed having the largest piece of the world's economic pie for so long. I suspect that if we are to compete successfully in the future international economy, major segments of our population will have to endure a virtual cultural change. They will have to study, think, and work considerably harder than they have for generations.

Furthermore, our savings rate as a nation has never been very good, and it has been declining over the past couple of decades. Currently, it is less than 5% in the United States, or less than one-quarter of Japan's savings rate. Our savings provide the capital necessary for improving, building, and sustaining our productive resources. From a financial standpoint, running a nation, politically and economically, is somewhat akin to running a very large family —except that the government can postpone paying its debt. Critical to the future financial health and, therefore, the standard of living of our people as a whole is: (1) how much we save, and (2) how we invest those savings.

Government tax policies have a substantial impact on how investors both save and invest. Now, Congress has never promised that tax policies will be either consistent or economically benefi-cial. The only thing we can be sure of is that every time taxes change, the change will be labeled reform. To you, of course, the question becomes, what will be left after you pay your taxes and how will the government's new approach dictate how you should invest your savings.

An example of a tax policy having an impact on our savings rate is the Individual Retirement Account (IRA). My early reaction to the inception of the IRA was that it was a gift from a grateful Republican administration to grateful Republican voters, who immediately took advantage of the tax break. Three or four years later, however, a vast number of Americans from all walks of life were using the tax benefits of an IRA to build retirement assets, and the nation's savings rate increased. Frankly, the implications of the IRA were much broader than Congress or most Americans perceived. A good many Americans are beneficiaries of pension or profit-sharing plans, but very few people have any involvement in the decision-making process regarding how these funds are invested. In setting up their own IRAs, however, Americans had to make some true capitalistic choices. The first, of course, was to create the savings, and the second, most valuable, exercise was that of decid-ing how the IRA money should be invested. With the IRA, we were well on the way toward educating a broad number of Americans in a capitalistic fashion. Isn't it a pity that the IRA was effectively *reformed* out of existence for most Americans.

One example of how tax policy influences our investment patterns, both individual investors and the nation as a whole, is the capital gains tax rate. In the mid-1970s, when the U.S. economy was flat on its tail and capital raising for small, growing enterprises was virtually nonexistent, capital gains tax rates were at their highest levels, and the incentive for investors to take risks to produce capital gains was also almost nonexistent. Furthermore, Jimmy Carter had run for office with an explicit program to increase capital gains taxes right up to the ordinary income rates. Based on the theory that a capital gains tax differential would stimulate financing for small, growing companies—the companies that produced the new jobs—and a study from Data Resources Inc., which indicated that the government would recover its lost revenues from the tax differentials within a five-year span, Congress actually reduced capital gains taxes substantially through the Tax Act of 1978.

Within a year, this country began its strongest period of risk-taking capital formation for small, growing companies and venture capital investments, thereby producing an expanding economy, a growth in jobs, and an increased prosperity for the nation. Within two years, the lost revenues to the government from the differential were restored, and Congressmen went home to win reelection by voicing their brilliant discovery that taxes could be reduced while actually increasing government revenues and providing a much-needed stimulus to the economy.

After the Tax Act of 1986, which unfortunately once again eliminated the capital gains tax differential, we Americans immediately became more conservative, the number of initial public offerings for small, growing companies peaked promptly and then substantially declined, and the number of Americans devoting their savings to interest-bearing accounts increased enormously while those who assumed risks for growth and appreciation decreased enormously. Congress has never quite understood Abe Lincoln's admonition that "you don't make the poor richer by making the rich poorer." If you take away the incentives for workers to work, they will not work. If you take away the incentives for investors to incur risk, they will not incur risk.

I am not advocating that we use tax policy to protect the rich; I believe we should use tax policy to encourage the rich to take risks with their investments. In fact, a good tax policy will give a very broad-based number of people a feeling that they can win by taking risks with their savings. A Robin Hood approach in tax policy will not work for the betterment of all. When we create an environment in which people assume risks with their savings, we are using these savings to create new products, services, and jobs, which in turn will provide more tax revenues for the government. That's when we have a win/win government policy

Fitting yourself, both philosophically and in practice, into this political and economic framework is a worthwhile place to start considering your investment policy. If I sound like a dedicated capitalist to you, I am. However, I admit that we have not yet created a world of equal opportunity. Nevertheless, as a substitute, we should not attempt to create a world of equal results through governmental redistribution of wealth. Having created a system motivated by incentives, we must certainly recognize that not everybody wins. Therefore, one of the concepts that more successful people are adopting is a feeling of responsibility to the less fortunate. I believe these programs to help people who need help are necessary but are also more effective in the private sector than they are when administered by the government. Therefore, as you contemplate your investment approach, I suggest that you make one of your consistent *investments* a portion of your time and your money to help those who are less successful.

Our political and economic systems are intertwined, and together they provide the uniqueness of this country. In an increasingly complex world of international competition, our first problem is to gain an understanding of the issues, our strengths, and our needs. Some of our competitors seem to understand our system better than we do. Ask yourself what a foreign visitor to our country regards as the outstanding attribute of our political system, and I bet the answer is: "Freedom of the individual." Ask a foreign visitor what he regards as the outstanding attribute of our economic system, and I bet that he answers: "The opportunity for a high standard of living." This is why we are so lucky. The joy of political freedom combined with the opportunity for a high standard of living is the best possible world for the individualist and the investor, and we have it.

•

It's Now 2001, and We're Still Lucky...

Most of you are very fortunate in that you have never had to listen to me talk: I talk a lot. As readers, you have the luxury to skim, skip, daydream, even nap. When I talk, I try to be as far away from home as possible. Years ago I learned that our credibility increases in direct proportion to our distance from home, except New Yorkers, who have credibility only with other New Yorkers, and people from Washington, D.C., who don't have credibility anywhere. When I give talks I almost always allow myself a few minutes of personal philosophy, occasionally related to the subject on which I am speaking.

Once I gave a talk to a somewhat elderly group of ladies and was on my way out with the chairman when she handed me an envelope. I asked, "What's this?" She told me it was a very small honorarium. I handed it back to her and said, "I'm a great believer in freedom of speech and certainly exercise it, so you take this back." She thanked me profusely and then asked whether she could put it into a new fund that they had just started. My response was, "Sure, what's your new fund?" She said, "Well, we've just started a fund to get better speakers."

If you understood clearly the concepts of our economic and political systems mentioned in chapter one, you probably have a better understanding of how our nation works than 95% of your fellow Americans. Nevertheless, my personal grade on the original chapter one was a C, with the conviction that a few of the things I mentioned were very important and a few were not.

Among the expressed ideas that strike me as valid a decade later: We may be the only nation in the world created from ideas, created from concepts of how our economic and political systems should work. We were not simply conquered or assumed, we were created by thought. The political concept is simply that we as individuals have a right to freedom, self-expression, and self-government. In our economic system, we as individuals have the right to pursue a high standard of living and enjoy it if we attain it. Remember that no other combination of political and economic systems promises both of these wonderful aspects of a good and happy life.

The responsibility of our government, once elected, is to make decisions, presumably on behalf of all of us. The function of our economic system is to produce goods and services for our people. We evaluate our economy on how well these things are done (for example, in producing heaps of goods and services). When our economy doesn't perform well (depression or recession), more and more people endorse alternative political approaches to improve the economy (usually socialistic in nature). Our economy has been the most productive in the history of the modern world, and all alternatives have been far less effective. Despite this performance, substantial numbers of our citizens still advocate more government control or ownership. The basic difference between a liberal and a conservative centers on the functions of the government, how much influence and control it should have on our lives and our business.

Major changes take time. The belief, however, that a nation can transform itself overnight from an unsuccessful collectivist economy into a thriving private enterprise system is wishful thinking. It takes years to grow a successful company, so it is not surprising that some of the nations who abandoned communism in 1989 are still struggling economically in 1999.

One of my convictions, therefore one of my windmills for decades, is the belief that the more education we get, the more likely we are to understand the wonders of our system and the less likely we are to turn to the government for a solution for our problems. Further, we'll elect better representatives.

I don't think I gave you very clear reasons why I so strongly believe you, the investor, should have this broad background clearly in mind. Let me try to be more convincing:

1. We're now living in a world in which common stock investing is more a norm than an unusual activity. Even today, however, most of our high schools do not provide economic education. Buying stocks with your savings is a more complex activity than simply putting money in your savings account. As a result, millions of people who are buying stocks today with alacrity regard them only as dollar amounts that go up and down in the daily newspaper instead of thinking of themselves as owners of a productive unit in our economic system. With education we make better investment choices, and with knowledge we build conviction on the choices we make.

2. Understanding how our system works allows us to convert daydreams into reasonable expectations or economic goals for ourselves.

3. If I am right when I buy a stock, I will help the economy as well as myself. This seems to help me psychologically when my stock is nosediving.

4. We Americans are so lucky; we have so much for which to be thankful, but most of us really do not even know why we should be so thankful. I regard my freedom of expression as one of the most precious attributes of my world. It took me only a month in the army to realize how precious freedom of expression is to me.

This seems an appropriate time to touch on the changes that have occurred in our economic and political worlds over the last decade. Certainly I am thankful I did not try to write a book forecasting our economy, because our economic success as a nation has been beyond my wildest dreams. Ten years ago we were still greatly concerned that Germany and Japan would be the big winners in the competitive "one world" economy we were creating. Yet we Americans are now economically so far ahead that it is really *our world.* Over this decade we have reduced unemployment to the point that we are now worrying about having enough skilled workers. Our inflation rate during the late 1990s has been so low that we hardly even think about it. Certainly the investor has had a ball. The Dow Jones Average during the 1990s has more than tripled.

I don't know that we have improved our government a whit, although prosperity has produced higher levels of tax revenues and the proximity of a balanced federal budget. From time to time, a concept or approach toward improving the government is both presented and endorsed and then subsequently defeated by the politicians (term limits, for example). If possible, our system of justice is even worse than a decade ago, since it is now more costly and slower than ever and makes worse decisions than ever. An observant lawyer friend once told me that breakdowns in a system of justice are not unheard of in history and that people begin to invent substitutes. Arbitration has been a fast-growing industry in our country for the last decade.

The stock market has been so ebullient and surprising in the 1990s. Sometimes I ask myself why it is so and why I did not foresee it more clearly. If I were asked to give a single reason for our success, it would be the amazing contribution technology has made to American business, our competitive position, and the enhancement of productivity in producing goods and services for our people. If I were allowed two reasons, the second would be an almost universal decision on the part of American corporate managements to make their companies competitive in the world economy. They certainly succeeded. It deeply hurt our sensitivities to eliminate enormous numbers of middle-management jobs, but we are pretty well through this process today. Many of these middle managers were actually forced into more productive jobs and therefore into making more substantial economic contributions.

Don't let my joy in America's economic success of the 1990s cover up the fact that I am a cranky old man with plenty of criticisms of American modern life. America is on a materialistic "roll" stemming from good pay, high employment, and the bubbly stock market. I am much disturbed that our savings rate in this country has actually become negative (−1.2%, June 1999) and represents the worst savings rate we have shown in 60 years of keeping statistics. Evidence abounds that our culture today centers on our individual welfare without too much concern for others or the rest of the world. We have certainly endorsed "freedom" in practically every construction we can give the word. Evidence of people accepting all the responsibilities for their freedom is a lot harder to find. Our personal debts have increased at an alarming rate. It seems at times that our moral and ethical standards have deteriorated about as rapidly as our ability to consume has increased. If this is so, then we face the real challenge of creating a nation with a revitalized culture as well as the historic educational challenges.

CHAPTER 2

Economics 101

BEFORE WE BEGIN TO BUILD OUR INVESTMENT POLICY, LET'S spend a few more moments examining basic economic concepts. I will define the concepts, then provide my viewpoint. Compare your own viewpoint with mine. If you think along with me, my hope is that you will develop a feel for financial issues. Like most worthwhile efforts in life, personal investing requires setting goals and then devising a way to achieve them.

It is my belief that each of us has an individual pattern of handling our finances and that we Americans generally have a rather unsophisticated concept of money and savings. In our early education, we are given some idea of the sanctity of a dollar as a dollar, and we hear that "a penny saved is a penny earned." I understand a Boy Scout is still supposed to be thrifty, in addition to his other sterling attributes, but, after that, the concept is not developed much. Presumably, in our formative years, we are taught something at home about handling money, a questionable schooling when we consider that our parents probably never had a course in handling money either.

After we study Ben Franklin in Boy Scouts, we go to college with an increasing tendency to focus on how we will make a living or prepare for grad school. When I was in college, I felt that all the really smart kids majored in English and all the really dumb kids majored in history. I figured I was not in either group, so I majored in economics. In terms of helping me handle my financial affairs in later life, I might as well have majored in music. No respectable liberal arts college permits a mundane course in money management for the individual. Many of our young people, therefore, are taught how to make a good living, but are not taught how to manage themselves financially while they are making this good living. As a result, they become doctors or lawyers or even stockbrokers (if they can't do anything else), but they are not taught how to build their assets. Managing money, that is, how to save and how to invest, is a subject left either to instinct or the first good salesman who comes along.

I suspect that, unfortunately, what I have described is typical American financial training. We have some awareness that we should save and that we should invest those savings wisely, but we do not think much about it, let alone plan. Therefore, let's go back to the basics.

Money

In economics courses, *money* is defined very simply as a *medium of exchange*. Having some with you is convenient, so you can exchange it (buy something). We work for it, we use it to pay our bills, we invest it, but what we are really doing is exchanging it. We speak of people as having a lot of money, but what we are really saying is that they are wealthy. Cary Grant made a lot of money but reportedly never carried more than $50 in cash. Maybe we can go to the bank and borrow a lot of money, but when we do, this borrowed money is not part of our savings and it does not make us any wealthier. If I asked you whether you would like to have a lot of money, you would say, "Sure," but what you really mean is that you would like to have a lot of savings and be wealthy. Let's quit thinking about money—it is not important unless you do not have any.

Savings (the Noun)

In economics courses, *savings*, the noun, is defined as *deferred spending*. This definition implies that all the money we have will eventually be spent, if not by ourselves, then perhaps by our children, and almost certainly by our grandchildren. Those of us who have been taught to save do not like to think this is true, even though it probably is. The deferred-savings concept is an interesting one to consider for a moment because it introduces the time element in your investment policy. Have you seriously considered the period of time in which you are going to be investing your savings? For example, do you have a finite period of years before you retire? Or maybe you are designing your investment policy for your lifetime. How long is that? To help you answer this question, take a look at table 2.1. It is a simple life expectancy table, which will give you an idea of how long you are likely to live. An interesting couple of dates to keep in mind are how long you are expected to live and how long it is till you retire. The time period between the two will have investment implications for you.

If you think the questions I am raising about the time element in investing are simplistic, let me give you a couple of examples of major investment mistakes stemming directly from a lack of financial training made by enormous numbers of older Americans. One mistake many older Americans make is to become very conservative in their investing when they retire, and then suffer from a decline in their standard of living as inflation erodes their savings' purchasing power and they live longer than they expected. The second mistake many senior Americans make stems from their belief that they should never invade principal. As a result, in order to maintain their income stream, they take greater and greater risks with investments to produce higher rates of return and end up losing substantial chunks of that principal.

Just pause for a moment and think about the time element for you in terms of your saving and your investing that comes from the concept of deferred spending.

Table 2.1

Life Expectancy

Present Age	Life Expectancy (Number of Years)		Present Age	Life Expectancy (Number of Years)	
	Males	Females		Males	Females
20	52.1	56.7	50	25.5	29.6
21	51.1	55.8	51	24.7	28.7
22	50.2	54.9	52	24.0	27.9
23	49.3	53.9	53	23.2	27.1
24	48.3	53.0	54	22.4	26.3
25	47.4	52.1	55	21.7	25.5
26	46.5	51.1	56	21.0	24.7
27	45.6	50.2	57	20.3	24.0
28	44.6	49.3	58	19.6	23.2
29	43.7	48.3	59	18.9	22.4
30	42.8	47.2	60	18.2	21.7
31	41.9	46.5	61	17.5	21.0
32	41.0	45.6	62	16.9	20.3
33	40.0	44.6	63	16.2	19.6
34	39.1	43.7	64	15.6	18.9
35	38.2	42.8	65	15.0	18.2
36	37.3	41.9	66	14.4	17.5
37	36.5	41.0	67	13.8	16.9
38	35.6	40.0	68	13.2	16.2
39	34.7	39.1	69	12.6	15.6
40	33.8	38.2	70	12.1	15.0
41	33.0	37.3	71	11.6	14.4
42	32.1	36.5	72	11.0	13.8
43	31.2	35.6	73	10.5	13.2
44	30.4	34.7	74	10.1	12.6
45	29.6	33.8	75	9.6	12.1
46	28.7	33.0	76	9.1	11.6
47	27.9	32.1	77	8.7	11.0
48	27.1	31.2	78	8.3	10.5
49	26.3	30.4	79	7.8	10.1
			80	7.5	9.6

Source: Internal Revenue Code

WEALTH

Economically, wealth can be equated with savings, but it is worth-while to think of what *wealthy* means to you. Can you put a dollar figure on it? My personal definition of wealthy is having enough money to do most everything you want to do. This definition varies the figure for each of us. When we were kids, I can remember my buddies and I expressing our desire to be *rich* like one of our friends, who seemed to be able to buy a Coke whenever he wanted and, therefore, was regarded as the rich kid in the neighborhood. As we grow older, wealthy becomes somewhat of a moving target even though we still have a tendency to attach some finite figure to it. Certainly, anybody with $1 million in my childhood days was almost unheard of. What seems like only a few years ago, there were about 20,000 millionaires in the United States. Very recently, I saw an article indicating that there are now 1 million millionaires in our country. Even in real dollars, that's a large increase. Apparently, being wealthy is a moving target nationally as well. Anyway, I figure that if we have enough money to do most everything we want, we are wealthy.

Emotionally, I think most Americans regard as wealthy all people who have more than they themselves. We do not think of ourselves as wealthy. Wealthy starts just above us. Some years ago at a speech in Chicago before a securities industry group, I made the mistake of referring to all of us present as "stinking rich." I suspect we had had one or two good years in a row at that time. My friend Tubby Burnham, who was then chairman of Drexel Burnham, and who *is* stinking rich, picked up on it immediately with the comment that he hadn't realized I was stinking rich. Of course, compared to Tubby, I'm not, and wasn't, so about all I could do was observe that being wealthy is somewhat of a relative thing. Since feeling wealthy is presumably a pleasant feeling, I suggest that if we set our standards just below where we are instead of just above, we'll all feel marginally wealthy all the time.

On one of my too frequent trips to New York, the Plaza Hotel gave me a copy of *Town & Country*—there wasn't a magazine that month with one of the Trumps on the cover. I happened to read an article titled "Golden Apple," which described the 25 blocks of Fifth Avenue characterized as the "spacious and elegant" places to live. A real estate brokerage firm had conducted a demographic study of the occupants in this area. Almost 85% of the people were in finance, law, or medicine. They produced an average annual income of $470,800. Guess what their average net worth was? Well, it was only $3.1 million, a figure that implies to me that they can't afford to live there, or at least they'd better hang onto their jobs for a while!

The interesting philosophical question for each of us is to consider the intertwining of our pursuit of happiness and our pursuit of wealth, and perhaps make sure that we are achieving happiness at the same time we are pursuing wealth. I have known a few people to whom there is almost a direct correlation between money and happiness. Therefore, happiness seems to revolve around getting more money. The best that can be said for this approach is that it does not lead to any confusions in goals. I am convinced that almost anyone who desires to be wealthier and is willing to make all the sacrifices necessary to do so, can be wealthier. Just before the crash of 1987, about 30% of the Harvard Business School graduates trooped off to New York City and the securities industry with the clear-cut goal of getting rich. What they got was a chance to live in New York City (a terrible place), ride the subway, and root for the Mets!

My generation had a tendency to be rather robotic in terms of wealth versus happiness. Too many of my friends are retiring as early as they can from jobs they really did not like to pursue happiness. Twenty-five years or so is a long time to spend doing something you do not enjoy. If you happen to have a job you truly love, even though it has low pay, you are probably better off than having a high-paying occupation that you abhor. One of the changes in the American culture from my generation to the next is that young people today do not have to be robots. Some of my friends do not like me talking to their offspring because I usually advocate that they quit their comfortable, miserable jobs and actively muddle toward an occupation that they thoroughly enjoy.

The correlation between wealth and happiness for most of us probably does not go very far up the money scale. Many might contend that, at the far end, being very, very wealthy leads to unhappiness. I am not sure that has to be so at all, although having many assets takes more time to manage well. Realize that being wealthy is usually a moving target for each of us and that it places more responsibilities upon us. Therefore, it is important to spend some time thinking about both the pursuit of happiness and the pursuit of wealth, how they fit together, and what responsibilities we take on as a result.

SAVING (THE VERB)

We all know what *saving* means. But really think about it. How does a person get wealthy? In terms of economics, the answer is easy: Create savings and invest your savings well. Some easy ways to create savings, of course, are to be born with it, marry it, or hit the lottery—all of which are statistically remote. For most of us, saving out of our income over a period of time is the only way to reach our goal of building wealth. Generally, young people have skinny balance sheets, and saving money thus has an enormous positive impact on their net worth.

Table 2.2, a convincing chart on the joys of saving, shows what $1,000 per year of savings will amount to over differing periods of years at differing rates of return. For example, if you save $1,000 a year for 20 years, and invest these savings to produce 12% per annum, all of a sudden (in 20 years) you'll have over $80,000. This is a rather compelling statistical case for being a saver.

Years ago at a securities industry convention, we were shown a 15-minute animated film called *The Richest Man in Babylon*. The theme is simple enough, and written at about the sixth-grade level, about right for us investment bankers and money managers. In ancient Babylon, the hero paid himself first every time he was paid, putting aside something like 10% out of every pay. With this

Table 2.2

Compound Interest

(Investment of $1,000 per Year, Compounded Annually)

Rate %	5 Years Total Invested $5,000	10 Years Total Invested $10,000	15 Years Total Invested $15,000	20 Years Total Invested $20,000	25 Years Total Invested $25,000	30 Years Total Invested $30,000
2	5,308	11,169	17,639	24,783	32,671	41,379
3	5,468	11,808	19,157	27,676	38,553	49,003
4	5,633	12,486	20,825	30,969	43,312	58,328
5	5,802	13,207	22,657	34,719	50,113	70,761
6	5,975	13,972	24,673	38,992	58,156	83,802
7	6,153	14,784	26,888	43,865	67,676	101,073
8	6,336	15,645	29,324	49,423	78,954	122,346
9	6,523	16,560	32,003	55,765	92,324	148,575
10	6,716	17,531	34,950	63,002	108,182	180,943
11	6,913	18,561	38,190	71,265	126,999	220,913
12	7,115	19,654	41,754	80,699	149,334	270,292
13	7,322	20,815	45,672	91,470	175,850	331,315
14	7,535	22,044	49,980	103,769	207,333	406,737
15	7,754	23,350	54,718	117,810	244,712	499,957
16	7,977	24,733	59,925	133,841	289,088	615,161
17	8,207	26,120	65,649	152,139	341,762	757,503
18	8,442	27,755	71,939	173,021	404,272	933,318
19	8,683	29,404	78,850	196,847	478,431	1,150,387
20	8,930	31,150	86,442	224,026	566,377	1,418,258

Source: Johnson's Charts 1991

disciplined approach to saving, he ended up being "the richest man in Babylon," and presumably happy. This was probably the most convincing movie the securities industry ever sponsored. It is also available in paperback and worth careful reading. You probably know somebody who has saved like this. I had a friend, a carpenter with a wife and two kids, who saved something from his pay every month. He never made a lot of money, but he paid himself first and invested his savings well, compounded them well, and became *wealthy*.

Americans as a group, however, are not very good savers. As I mentioned before, we manage to save between 3% and 5% of our annual income. That is less than it was 20 years ago. The Japanese, on the other hand, have been saving 20% or more of their income for decades. When savings are reinvested, they have an enormously favorable impact on the economy of the nation. The important competitive questions are how much is saved and how these savings are invested.

One of my many unproven theories is that our personal pattern of saving is set at a very early age. Some of us are savers and some are spenders. An objective observer can usually tell which way we lean by the time we are age seven. From then on, we are only amending our behavior. Can you change your savings pattern? If your response is yes and you intend to do it, the odds are overwhelmingly against you. But, with vigilance and commitment, you can overcome those odds.

Frankly, I do not know how our individual saving and spending patterns are established, because the variations even within the same family appear to be substantial. Presumably, each of our children has the same upbringing and yet their saving patterns differ greatly. I have seen this in my own urchins from an early age. There are three of them with patterns that seem to be as follows:

• *First Urch:* You get money by working for it and you should do this, because eating well is important, but you should not work past the opening kickoff. Furthermore, spending should not be deferred.

- *Second Urch*: You get money by working for it and everyone should do this. Once you have some money, it's okay to give it away to others, but you should not spend much on yourself and you should save.
- *Third Urch*: You get money by working for it, but you should work for enjoyment, not money. You should also bear in mind, however, that money is nothing more than a medium of exchange and should be immediately exchanged for some material good, which may or may not last longer than a dollar bill.

Where do you fit into this question of saver versus spender? Do you see yourself in one of these patterns, or do you have another, different pattern? If you would like to change, can you do it? Since becoming wealthy involves creating savings and investing them well, let me throw out a few further observations on the psychological aspects of savers and spenders, and you relate them to yourself.

Good savers do not necessarily make good investors. Of course, neither do good spenders. Good savers, however, remain good savers under most economic conditions and almost never have a real financial problem. I have never met one who did. Sometimes I think that it does not even matter what good savers earn; they will save something under any economic conditions. Probably, this is because good savers generally require of themselves that they have the money before they buy something. You would think they would have greater peace of mind than good spenders, but that does not seem to be necessarily so. Since good spenders frequently spend before they have the money, they usually have a higher cost of living in the form of interest charges on their debts, but their peace of mind seems only to be disturbed when their spending gets completely out of hand. Most of us would like to save better than we do, but we do not seem to change much even when we take the oath, set up a budget, and try to live by it.

Remember, I am asking these questions with the hopes of building some practical goals. I think we can amend ourselves somewhat, but if we try to change ourselves completely, it probably will not work.

It is important to recognize what approach is practical for us and then adopt this approach wholeheartedly. I once had a client with a very clear, well-defined investment objective. Her husband had died and left her $3 million, and her objective was to spend the last dime on the day she died. About all I could do was show her a mortality table and give her some reasonable expectations of income while she lived. Her problem, of course, was that we did not know when she was going to die. At the rate she spent, however, there was a pretty good probability that the last dime would go before she did.

INFLATION

Most Americans learn early about inflation—by the time they are old enough to buy bubble gum for a couple of years. Certainly, we can remember our mothers lamenting the exorbitant prices of bacon and eggs at almost any point in our childhood. It is interesting that this idea of inflation always expresses a regret that prices are going up instead of a lament that the value of our money is going down. Keep in mind that it is not money that counts; it is the purchasing power of that money that is important. After we have learned either to make it or spend it, the most important concept of money is that it changes in value. Furthermore, it generally declines in value over time. The rate of inflation is worth keeping clearly in mind as a backdrop to both savings and investment. Our early training on the sanctity of the dollar and the relatively gradual rate of American inflation over the last 40 years makes us a little more sanguine about inflation than we should be.

Europeans seem to have a better concept of inflation than Americans. I will never forget a call from a foreign-born, well-educated client in the summer of 1974, a period of 12% inflation and a terrible stock market. His comment was: "Dave, you Americans are crazy."

I replied: "I know, but specifically how?"

His response was very telling: "For the first time in your lives you see inflation and you run out and put your money in the bank."

What he was saying was that in a period of rapid inflation we Americans were more interested in protecting our dollars than our purchasing power.

Another very bright business school friend of mine was Czechoslovakian. He was about 12 years old in 1938 when the Germans rolled in. His father was killed, but his family had some money in the bank. At age 12, he took the family savings out of the bank and invested in the one material good purchasable in quantity—book matches. Inflation was so rampant that, by converting his money to a material good, he saved his family's purchasing power and eventually bought his way to America.

Table 2.3 shows changes in the cost of living annually from 1938 through 1990. As you look at the figures, it is difficult to comprehend that South American countries have inflation rates of 50% to 100% a year. In Germany after World War I, you could put enough money in the bank at the beginning of the year to buy a car and take the same amount out at the end of the year to buy a loaf of bread. Spend a little time with this table, kids. What it really shows is how much your assets had to increase at the end of one year, five years, or ten years to be as well off as you were at the start of the period.

It is somewhat comforting that since 1938 the U.S. cost of living increased as much as 10% in only four years. Unfortunately, the cost of living actually declined in only three years, each of them less than 2%. What really counts, of course, is what happens over a period of time. Even at our moderate rates of inflation, you can see from the chart that the cost of living increased 57% for the five years ending in 1982 or 129% for the ten years ending in 1982. Translated, this means that the American individual or family had to have 129% more money at the end of 1982 than ten years previously just to be as well off as before. It is in this context that we place the challenge to saving and investing. If we stay the same, we lose.

What rate of inflation per year would be acceptable to you for the rest of your life? What rate of inflation do you think you will have for the rest of your life? These are tough questions. Some people read bar charts better than they read figures. I worry enough about inflation to be a bit redundant and include the bar chart as table 2.4, which translates the same inflation figures annually and in five- and ten-year periods. Bar charts are good for watching waves. If you want to be scared, you can visualize the building of the next wave.

Back in 1979, I remember asking a group of students what inflation rate they would accept for the rest of their lives. Since the rate of inflation at that time was around 12%, the overwhelming consensus was that 8% per year for their lives would be satisfactory. Table 2.3 shows that the mid-1980s had an average inflation rate of 4.3%. None of us, including economists, knows what will happen in the next decade. As one simplistic approach to this question, ask yourself how likely it is that our Congress will balance the budget and begin to reduce the national debt. When I ask myself this question, I end up wondering how bad inflation really could be over the next decade.

For the saver/investor, there is a very simple and handy guide to getting a feel for the ravages of inflation on your assets as well as a feel for the savings or investment results necessary to combat it. It's called the rule of 72. I have no idea why *72* is the magic number, but it is great for telling us how long it will take to double our money at various rates of return. I will give you four illustrations:

1. If I make 8% a year on my assets, how long will it be before they double? 9 years (72 divided by 8% equals 9 years)
2. If inflation is 6% a year, how long will it be before my current assets drop to half in purchasing power, or I must double my assets to maintain my purchasing power? 12 years (72 divided by 6% equals 12 years)
3. Let's get a little fancy. If inflation is 6% and I can compound my assets at 8%, how long will it be before I have doubled my purchasing power? 36 years (8% return minus 6% inflation equals 2%, 72 divided by 2% equals 36 years)
4. We are getting pretty good, so let's show off. If somebody tells you they doubled their money in six years in a certain stock, you can look very bright momentarily by responding, "Oh, you got 12%-a-year compounded. Not bad." (72 divided by 6 years equals 12%)

Table 2.3

U.S. Cost of Living (1947–1999)

Year	Dec. Index 1982–84 = 100	% Yearly Change	5-Year Change	5-Year Average Rate of Inflation	10-Year Change	10-Year Average Rate of Inflation
1946	21.5	—	—	—	—	—
1947	23.4	9.0%	38.7%	6.8%	62.5%	5.0%
1948	24.1	2.7	38.1	6.7	71.7	5.6
1949	23.6	–1.8	32.8	5.8	69.4	5.4
1950	25.0	5.8	37.4	6.6	77.5	5.9
1951	26.5	5.9	23.1	4.2	71.3	5.5
1952	26.7	0.9	14.0	2.7	58.1	4.7
1953	26.9	0.6	11.7	2.2	54.2	4.4
1954	26.7	–0.5	13.1	2.5	50.3	4.2
1955	26.8	0.4	7.3	1.4	47.5	4.0
1956	27.6	2.9	4.3	0.9	28.4	2.5
1957	28.4	3.0	6.5	1.3	21.4	1.9
1958	28.9	1.8	7.7	1.5	20.2	1.9
1959	29.4	1.5	9.9	1.9	24.3	2.2
1960	29.8	1.5	11.1	2.1	19.2	1.8
1961	30.0	0.7	8.7	1.7	13.4	1.3
1962	30.4	1.2	6.8	1.3	13.8	1.3
1963	30.9	1.6	6.7	1.3	14.9	1.4
1964	31.2	1.2	6.4	1.3	16.9	1.6
1965	31.8	1.9	6.8	1.3	18.7	1.8
1966	32.9	3.4	9.7	1.9	19.2	1.8
1967	33.9	3.0	11.6	2.2	19.2	1.8
1968	35.5	4.7	15.0	2.8	22.7	2.1
1969	37.7	6.1	20.6	3.8	28.3	2.5

Year					
1970	39.7	5.5	24.8	4.5	33.4	2.9
1971	41.1	3.4	24.8	4.5	36.9	3.2
1972	42.5	3.4	25.3	4.6	39.7	3.4
1973	46.2	8.8	30.2	5.4	49.7	4.1
1974	51.9	12.2	37.6	6.6	66.0	5.2
1975	55.5	7.0	39.6	6.9	74.3	5.7
1976	58.2	4.8	41.6	7.2	76.8	5.9
1977	62.1	6.8	46.2	7.9	83.2	6.2
1978	67.7	9.0	46.5	7.9	90.7	6.7
1979	76.7	13.3	47.9	8.1	103.6	7.4
1980	86.2	12.4	55.4	9.2	117.0	8.1
1981	93.9	8.9	61.4	10.1	128.5	8.6
1982	97.6	3.9	57.2	9.5	129.8	8.7
1983	101.3	3.8	49.6	8.4	119.1	8.2
1984	105.3	4.0	33.3	5.9	103.1	7.3
1985	109.3	3.8	26.7	4.8	96.9	7.0
1986	110.5	1.1	17.6	3.3	90.0	6.6
1987	115.4	4.4	18.1	3.4	85.8	6.4
1988	120.6	4.4	19.1	3.6	78.1	5.9
1989	126.1	4.6	19.8	3.7	64.4	5.1
1990	133.8	6.1	22.4	4.1	55.2	4.5
1991	137.9	3.1	24.8	4.5	46.9	3.9
1992	141.9	2.9	23.0	4.2	45.4	3.8
1993	145.8	2.7	20.9	3.9	43.9	3.7
1994	149.7	2.7	18.7	3.5	42.2	3.6
1995	153.5	2.5	14.7	2.8	40.4	3.5
1996	158.6	3.3	15.0	2.8	43.5	3.7
1997	161.3	1.7	13.7	2.6	39.8	3.4
1998	163.9	1.6	12.4	2.4	35.9	3.6
1999	168.3	2.7	12.4	2.4	33.5	3.4

Source: Johnson's Charts

Table 2.4
U.S. Inflation (Cost of Living Increase: 1951–1999)

Annual Rate, Year by Year

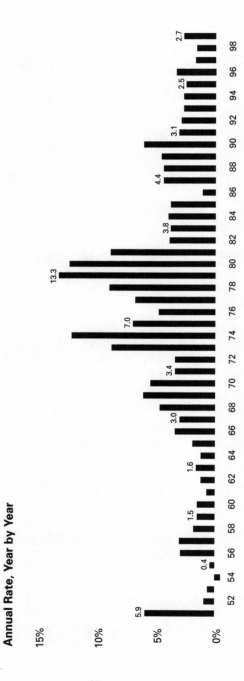

Annual Rate, 5-Year Period

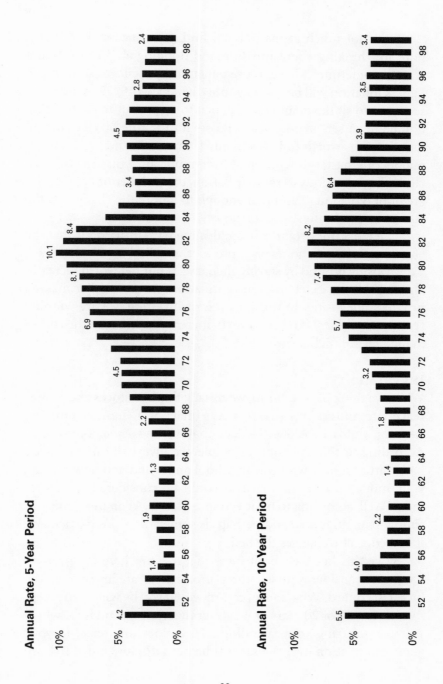

Annual Rate, 10-Year Period

I am not much at math, but I find this concept very handy, both for thinking about inflation and thinking about investment results. Sometimes I have to use paper and pencil. For example, if I guess inflation will be 5%, I cannot divide 5% into 72 in my head, so I have to sit down and use a pencil to figure out that I had best double my assets in 14.4 years. Fuss with the rule of 72 until you have it—it is worth it. It is a handy framework, and even English majors can master the concept. More important, you will also conclude that in periods of rapid inflation, the number of people who are both old enough and rich enough to ignore the changes in the cost of living diminishes enormously.

The most important concept dealing with inflation is that the changing value of money as a product of inflation simply means we are losing ground by staying the same. If our net worth increases annually by the exact amount of inflation, we are neither making progress nor losing. In this business of investing, we are winning (getting wealthier) if our net worth increases faster than the cost of living. Restful nights ensue.

INVESTMENT

When we think of *investment*, we usually think of stocks and bonds, real estate, and savings accounts. As a final bow to basic economics, we might also consider the fact that *savings equal investment*. According to this textbook principle, we invest all our savings. I had a little trouble with this in school and wondered how putting your money under the mattress could be considered an investment. Well, according to basic economics, it is. As an investment, it simply pays no return and perhaps is somewhat risky, particularly if someone else changes the bed.

Since this book is about investing, my aim here is simply to have you consider yourself for a moment as an investor in the broadest context. What rate of return would you be willing to accept for the next 10 or 20 years or whatever that time period is for which you are deferring your spendings? How does this relate to your guess on inflation over the same time period? How much risk are you willing to assume and how does that relate to your guess on rate of return? Needless to say, the higher the rate you pick, the more risk you have that you will not get it. The rule of 72 will tell you quickly how wealthy you will be at a future date if you invest your savings at different rates.

Look at table 2.5, which shows you how much money you will have if you start with $10,000 and apply your rate to it for 5, 10, or 20 years. It looks pretty good, doesn't it? If, for example, you pick 10%, you can see that your $10,000 will grow to $67,275 at the end of 20 years. If you pick a very high rate, you might consider that J. Paul Getty compounded his assets at only 17% annually. Of course, J. Paul lived a long time, longer than table 2.5 runs. If you like math, you could extend the table to 60 years, or you can just accept my word for the fact that it comes out to over $1 billion.

When you looked up the figure that gave you $67,275 at the end of 20 years, did you figure out what to do about taxes as you went along? The compounding table requires that you compound the whole thing; you cannot spend any of the income, even for taxes. That can be a bit difficult for even a good saver. Therefore, if you figure you are going to have to pay taxes out of the principal or income, you might reduce your guess by a couple of percentage points or so to allow for taxes. Let's say you now guess 8%, which means that after 20 years instead of having $67,275 you will have $46,610. Still not bad.

Wait a minute, did you adjust for inflation? Good grief. Well, there are several ways to do this, including the rule of 72, of course, but a quick way is to subtract your guess on the inflation rate from your guess on rate of return (after you have already subtracted taxes if you are going to pay them out of this pot), and simply read the chart to see how much better off you will be in terms of real wealth. For example, if you thought you could do 10% as a rate of return but need 2% for taxes, you're at 8%. If you guessed 5% for inflation, you're at 3%. At 3% you will more than double your savings in 25 years—but that seems like a long time.

Table 2.5

Compound Interest

(Investment of $10,000 per Year, Compounded Annually)

Rate %	5 Years	10 Years	15 Years	20 Years	25 Years	30 Years
2	$11,041	$12,190	$13,459	$14,859	$16,406	$18,114
3	11,593	13,439	15,580	18,061	20,938	24,273
4	12,167	14,802	18,009	21,911	26,658	32,434
5	12,763	16,289	20,789	265,533	33,864	43,219
6	13,382	17,908	23,966	32,071	42,919	57,435
7	14,026	19,672	27,590	38,697	54,274	76,123
8	14,693	21,589	31,722	46,610	68,485	100,627
9	15,386	23,674	36,425	56,044	86,231	132,677
10	16,105	25,937	41,772	67,275	108,347	174,494
11	16,851	28,394	47,846	80,623	135,855	228,923
12	17,623	31,058	54,736	96,463	170,001	299,599
13	18,424	33,946	62,543	115,231	212,305	391,159
14	19,254	37,072	71,379	137,435	264,619	509,501
15	20,114	40,456	81,371	163,665	329,189	662,118
16	21,003	44,114	92,655	194,608	408,742	858,498
17	21,924	48,068	105,387	231,056	506,578	1,110,646
18	22,878	52,338	119,737	273,930	626,686	1,433,706
19	23,864	56,947	135,895	324,294	773,881	1,846,753
20	24,883	61,917	154,070	383,376	953,962	2,373,763

Source: Johnson's Charts 1991

36

We should all recognize that *how* we acquire our savings has some pretty strong psychological impacts on our investment of these savings. High rates of return require the assumption of a fair degree of risk. If you work very hard to produce your savings in small increments, it is generally not very simple to become an aggressive investor. You might think about this for a moment and relate the question back to our consideration of the pursuit of happiness. If your tolerance for investment pain is low, your best alternative may be to be a good saver and a conservative investor.

Buck up, kids. As we think about these different concepts, I suspect that you are reaching the same conclusion I have—this business of managing our finances is a tough game. Thinking about ourselves relative to these various challenges, interrelationships, and trade-offs is not always a pleasant exercise, but it is a worthwhile step in establishing our own investment policy. We need some idea of our own goals; they have to be practical and realistic for us. The keys to economic well-being, however, are creating our savings and investing them well. The next time you are tempted to buy a get-rich-quick book, save your money and invest it.

•

Ten Years Later...

Certainly, from a historical perspective, the last decade has been the greatest period for creating wealth our country has ever known; lots of jobs, good pay, stable cost of living, declining interest rates, and a wonderful stock market. We can add to this the technology explosion that has created more than a few billionaires and heaps of millionaires. How have most Americans responded to this period?

Cynically and facetiously, I have interpreted the modern American approach as follows:

1. Our savings are no longer the money in our banks or securities. They include the unused balances on our credit cards. They are not what we owe, they are what our credit card companies and banks will still allow us to spend before they shut us off.

2. None of our savings actually comes from our income. We spend all of our income (as a matter of fact, we spend 101.2% of our income).

3. We do not worry about inflation because there isn't any worth mentioning at the moment, and we spend so fast that it wouldn't matter.

4. We buy "dot com" stocks, frequently with borrowed money, because the stock market only goes one way: up.

5. As our stocks go up, we will be able to borrow more money and spend even more.

6. Life's a ball!

Fortunately, we are not quite this bad. But it indicates the direction in which this country has moved. Part of our problem is that we Americans always believe that the present conditions in which we live will continue ad infinitum. They won't. I suspect my cynicism stems from the fact that I am a reasonably good saver. Good savers are annoyed by big spenders, just as big spenders are annoyed by good savers.

A confession: I mentioned those half-dozen economic terms, as simple as they were, to get you thinking about yourself relative to each, what they mean to you, and how they affect your life today and your goals for tomorrow. Let's keep thinking about you for a moment. "Money," "savings" (the noun), and "wealth" are inter-related and pertain to our assets. Do you currently consider your-self wealthy? If you are not, do you want to be? If you used a figure to define wealth, what would this figure be? How much does your feeling of wealth or poverty influence your happiness? Would you be considerably happier if you were wealthier? You've heard people say they would not have any problems if they had a million dollars. Is this true? Do you have a goal?

Now let's think about ourselves relative to "saving" (the verb), our awareness of inflation, and how we might approach the question of becoming wealthier. Probably all of us, if we really wanted, could become wealthier. I'll also contend there are very few of us who do in fact make a substantial (other than temporary) change in our approach toward saving or spending. With a little thought, however, we can understand ourselves, our nature, and what good and/or terrible things occur as a product of our saving and spending habits.

A second confession on my part is that the exhibit on compounding your money was included as a stimulus to savings. I am not equating the pursuit of wealth to the pursuit of happiness, but you might think about yourself relative to the pursuit of each and how each relates to you.

I worried enough about inflation ten years ago to include not one, but two tables on cost-of-living increases. Worth remembering is the fact that we could be worrying about it again in no time at all.

To become wealthier, we must either already have or must create savings and then make good investments. In the last 10 to15 years of the twentieth century, we Americans have become common stock investors, a monumental change. According to a recent survey, we expect a return between 14% and 19% annually on our common stocks. If we do this well, it will probably be more than double the increase in corporate earnings even in an excellent year for business. What do you think a realistic figure should be?

CHAPTER 3

Accounting 101

DO YOU KNOW HOW WEALTHY YOU ARE? I DO NOT MEAN generally; I mean precisely. We all have a general idea, but if we are going to invest well, we need rather specific numbers. Therefore, my aim, a veritable dedicated mission, is to have you create your personal balance sheet. Your balance sheet by definition is a snapshot of your financial condition at a given point in time—like today. It is a list of all your assets and all your liabilities. If you have created your balance sheet correctly, you can subtract your liabilities from your assets and determine your net worth—how wealthy you are. It is a very simple accounting formula:

$$\begin{array}{l} \text{Assets } (what\ we\ own) \\ - \text{ Liabilities } (what\ we\ owe) \\ \hline = \text{Net worth } (how\ wealthy\ we\ are) \end{array}$$

If you happen to be among the vast majority of Americans who have never actually sat down and created their own balance sheet, their listing of assets and liabilities, I will help you. As a matter of fact, I will spend four chapters (it is hoped, very brief) helping you, because we want to end up with a balance sheet that will be useful to you in establishing your investment policy and making financial decisions. Your balance sheet is the starting point, the focal point of your investment approach. If you have never made your balance sheet and I can convince you to do so, I will be happy for you.

Since I feel so strongly about it (I love a good balance sheet), let me convince you of the wonders and importance of creating your personal balance sheet. The conclusion is, of course, that you will be a happier, wealthier person for doing so—if not at the moment, certainly later on.

Let me count the ways:

1. Listing our assets and our liabilities tells us precisely where we are financially at this moment. At least we are mentally out of the fog and know with certainty what our financial situation is.
2. Our balance sheet will be the foundation for improving ourselves financially. It is the basis on which we will plan.
3. If you happen to use a financial adviser, he or she certainly has to know where you are currently, if you expect help on getting wealthier. Rare is the client who walks into my office and hands me a completed portfolio breakdown in such a fashion that we can immediately discuss alternative courses of action. The reverse is usually true. I have had clients with whom I spent the first six months of our association—part-time, thankfully—trying to determine exactly what the person's financial situation was. Sometimes this was a happy process. One client disclosed in our first meeting that she had $15,000 to invest, implying that this was about all the money she had in the world. A few months later we both had a clear picture of her balance sheet, which showed a net worth of well over $300,000.
4. If your balance sheet is the only financial record you keep and you revise it occasionally, the comparison of your new one with the old one will tell you whether you are getting richer or poorer. All you have to do is compare this year's net worth with last year's (you might adjust for inflation, of course). It's a scorecard.
5. Making up our balance sheet occasionally provides us with a psychological stimulus to improve our net worth. Periodic balance sheets can be an incentive to save, or at least to spend enough time with our financial affairs to improve our investment position.

6. It is very likely, once you have done your balance sheet, that you will discover assets with which you should do something. Frankly, I almost always discover something I should not have bought in the first place (and, therefore, something I probably should get rid of).

7. Your balance sheet is useful at income tax time, since practically all your financial assets and liabilities have some kind of tax implication. A quick check of your balance sheet will tell you if you forgot to include the $43.78 income you received on that savings account you started five years ago and have since neglected. Therefore, if you create a balance sheet, you will reduce the likelihood of going to jail.

Now, if you have never done this exercise, I will help you with your first balance sheet. We will make it as of the last day of this month, whatever this month is. In the future I suggest you use the dates June 30 and December 31. We could do it today, but we will wait till the end of the month, after payday, and before the bills come in, so your net worth will look better. As you know, I would like you to do your balance sheet twice a year, but I will settle for once a year in the future if you are dedicated to financial indigence. Before we start, let me give you a further note of encouragement. After you have done the first balance sheet, making them in the future gets to be a much easier process.

As a first step, and the only step for this chapter, take a look at table 3.1, which shows a long list of assets and liabilities. I present these only to jog your memory as to what some of your assets or liabilities may be. At the outset, you can scratch out all the ones you know you don't have and simply put down some estimates as to the money values of both assets and liabilities that you do have. My list is certainly not an all-inclusive one, so you may even think of assets or liabilities (assets, I hope) that you have, that I have not listed. Once you begin this process, put this fascinating book aside and calculate all your assets and liabilities precisely. For the moment, at least, forget all your small physical assets, your material goods.

Concentrate on the financial assets and liabilities and, if you like, very large physical assets like your home. The poorer you are the easier this should be and maybe the more important it is, especially if you want to quit being poor. The richer you are the harder it will be, but you will ultimately make some good decisions as a product of it. I don't care which you are. Just do it!

Having come this far, you can now subtract the total of your liabilities from the total of your assets to determine your net worth. If your net worth comes out to be less than zero, you're broke. Your investment policy, therefore, will be simply to figure out how to pay some of your debts so you can get back to zero and then increase your net worth from there.

If your net worth turns out to be more than you expected, congratulations. You're wealthier than you thought!

•

If You Do One Thing...

Making your own balance sheet (a list of your assets and liabilities) is the best advice offered in this book, particularly for those of you who don't now do it. Do it. It takes less work than you think, especially after you have done it once or twice. For those of us with computer capabilities, it gets easier all the time. Remember, you don't need to value all of your material goods, only the ones with substantial value.

In today's world, lots of you young kids have $2.80 in assets and plenty of debts. In today's world, if you are just out of college you could have $2.80 in assets and $100,000 in debts. Record them anyway. It will show you how deep you are in your financial hole and act as a stimulus for you to find ways to reduce your debt. Once you get back to ground level, Jack, you can start climbing the beanstalk to the sky.

It might be completely psychological, but people who do their balance sheets faithfully every six months seldom have serious financial problems. So do it.

Table 3.1

List of Assets and Liabilities

ASSETS

Liquid assets
Cash and checking account(s)
Savings account(s)
Money market funds
Life insurance cash values
U.S. savings bonds
Brokerage accounts cash/credit balance(s)
Other
    Total liquid assets

Marketable investments
Certificates of deposit
Municipal bonds
Corporate bonds
Mutual funds
Common stocks
Other
    Total marketable investments

Nonmarketable investments
Business interests
Investment real estate
Pension accounts
Profit-sharing accounts
Thrift plan accounts
IRA and other retirement plan accounts
Tax-sheltered Investments
Other
    Total nonmarketable investments

Personal real estate
Residence
Vacation home
    Total personal real estate

Table 3.1 *(continued)*
List of Assets and Liabilities

ASSETS *(continued)*

Other personal assets
Auto(s)
Boat(s)
Furs and jewelry
Collections, hobbies, etc.
Furniture and household accessories
Other personal property
   Total other personal assets
      Total assets

LIABILITIES

Current liabilities
Charge accounts, credit card charges, and other bills payable
Installment credit and other short-term loans
Unusual tax liabilities
   Total current liabilities

Long-term liabilities
Mortgage notes on personal real estate
Mortgage notes on investment real estate
Bank loans
Margin loans
Life insurance policy loans
Other
   Total long-term liabilities
      Total liabilities

      Family net worth

      Total liabilities and family net worth

CHAPTER 4

Lenders and Owners

So far in life, I have discovered only two ways to invest savings. The first is to lend them and the second is to use them to acquire ownership. Sounds pretty simple, doesn't it? So why would I dedicate a chapter to such a simple concept? The answer is equally simple: Too many people do not seem to care whether they lend or own; nor do they understand the implications of each, or else they believe that only one of the two ways is worth doing. In this chapter, we will see why lending and owning are *both* worth doing but for substantially different reasons.

A couple of years ago, a bright college kid, searching for a third way to invest, suggested *education* as an investment, with the implication that he would put it on his balance sheet. I am so much in favor of education that he stopped me for a moment before I could cynically respond that, in his case, the tuition was consumed and not invested. If he had insisted on *capitalizing* his education by putting it on his balance sheet and not on his resumé, I would have suggested that he list it under the heading of ownership, since I could not imagine anyone giving him his money back, never mind interest on his investment! So, we are still left with just lending and owning.

Let's discuss lending first. When we lend our money, we are essentially making a contract with the borrower, either directly or indirectly, in which the borrower promises to pay a set rate of return on our investment, until a finite date in the future at which time the lender receives his money back. The lender gets no more and no less than the contract specifies. We could make a long list of different fashions in which we make loans. We make a loan to the bank when we open a checking account or savings account. When we buy a bond, we are directly or indirectly making a loan to the institution that issued the bond. The borrower (or, debtor) can be a corporation, the U.S. government, a municipality, a federal agency, a bank, or even one of your buddies. Sometimes I think there are almost as many ways to make loans as there are ways to spend money.

The United States has historically been a nation of lenders. We dedicate the vast majority of our savings to lendings and almost all our liabilities are created by somebody lending us money. When someone lends us money, we have the same obligations as any of the borrowers I listed above: We pay a set rate of return for at least some period of time, and we promise to repay the face amount of the loan to the lender.

Though we like to think of our lendings as safe, they are certainly not without risk, most frequently when we think we have snared a high rate of return. There are two basic risks in lending: (1) credit risk, and (2) interest rate risk. Both of these risks should be kept clearly in mind when you buy a bond or make any type of loan.

Credit risk is the risk that we will not receive our interest payments or get our principal back from the borrower. It is a well-recognized risk, and we Americans have rightfully always worried about it, especially recently.

The second risk of lending, interest rate risk, stems from the fact that interest rates change during the period that we own the loan or bond, causing the market value of our loan to fluctuate while the loan is outstanding. Frankly, unlike credit risk, most Americans do not clearly recognize the impact that interest rate risk can have on the value of their fixed income investments. Therefore, worry about it for the moment, and I will get back to it a little later.

Acquiring ownership is usually a little more complicated than lending. In contrast to a loan, when you are an owner, nobody promises you anything. You are not promised that you will get a set rate of return (corporations are not legally required to pay you a dividend), and nobody promises to repay your money on any particular date in the future. To a great extent, owners get what is left over after the lenders have been paid. This can be a good situation or a much worse one if the company is really in trouble. In the bankruptcy arena, one of the many aspects about the court system that amazes me is why the common stock shareholders, the owners, get anything in a bankruptcy when the lenders have not gotten everything to which they are entitled. The cynical answer, of course, is because these legal machinations are settled by our court system.

Before we get into the details of the wonders of ownership, I would like you to do a little mental exercise. Take a look at the list of assets and liabilities in your balance sheet, which you whipped right off as a product of reading the last chapter, and divide the list of items into either *lendings* or *ownership*. What percentage of your assets represents lendings and what percentage ownership? In the next chapter, we will break down ownership into more detailed categories. First, let's explore the kinds of ownership that exist in our world.

I have discovered only three ways in which to acquire ownership as an investment. The first is to invest in (not consume) material goods. The second is to acquire ownership of real estate. The third way is to buy common stocks. We will briefly discuss each type of ownership.

MATERIAL GOODS

We consume most of the material goods we purchase, and when we do, we are not making an investment of our savings. Each of us can certainly justify a pleasing purchase with the observation that the price was so good it was a worthwhile *investment*. The fact is, however, that we spent the money. As I have mentioned, we Americans spend more than 95% of our income. We are good consumers and lousy savers. We all know a few people, however, who actually invest substantial portions of their savings in material goods, frequently with the idea of enjoying the asset, but primarily with the aim of having these goods appreciate in value.

For a moment, why don't we think of someone we know who does material goods investing very well. Certainly, a lot of us did a better job of buying baseball cards or postage stamps when we were kids than we do buying material goods as adults. The biggest threats to us kids, of course, were our mothers, who threw away these appreciating assets while filling the attic with worthless copies of *National Geographic.* Incidentally, I had a good mother, who left my cards alone. *I* am the one who lost my 1935 "Arky" Vaughan card.

I am sure you can think of some friends who own some valuable antiques. In the little New England town in which my wife grew up, an ex-high-school teacher has become a rather renowned expert on American antiques. I am not about to advise him how to invest his money; he does it quite well already. Essentially, he acquires ownership of a material good at an attractive price and either maintains his ownership as it appreciates or he sells it. When he sells it, it is generally at an even more attractive price.

How about art? Another friend of mine, who ran a very successful Wall Street securities firm, attended his first art auction at Sotheby's in London some years ago in search of an entertaining evening. He had one, and he bought a painting. Subsequently, he went to a couple of auctions a year because they were fun. He recently told me that he had made far more money buying Impressionist paintings than he had ever made from his investments on Wall Street. Pretty good material goods investing.

Now, for most of us, these illustrations on material goods investing are somewhat unique. Many of us *collect* certain items, but the value of our material goods generally has little impact on our balance sheet or on our investment process. I do not want you to use our discussion of physical assets as an excuse for not doing your financial balance sheet. My suggestion, therefore, is that most of us can forget about material goods as important items on our semiannual balance sheet. Unless we are serious collectors or in a material goods business, the existence of these assets is not going to have much influence on our investment policy or strategy. You make your own judgment, but I generally just pretend my material goods are worthless. If our physical assets survive the onslaught of our children, we can figure that the grandbrats will finish them off.

REAL ESTATE

Real estate is a second approach to acquiring ownership as an investment. As a matter of fact, if someone were to ask me what successful investment a very substantial number of Americans have made in the last 25 years, I would say it has been the purchase of their own home. They may have bought the home as a place to live and not with an orientation toward appreciation, but, nevertheless, substantial appreciation in value occurred over time for many homeowners. Furthermore, since most Americans cannot afford to pay for homes immediately in one lump sum, we leverage this ownership asset through a mortgage, frequently inspired by the tax deductibility of the interest, and thereby produce an excellent return on our original equity over a period of years. Despite the recent difficulties in the real estate market, I have a favorable leaning toward home ownership. First, even if the home does not appreciate, paying off the monthly mortgage can be a forced savings that many people otherwise would not make. Second, once we own our homes, most of us spend some of our income improving them. To whatever extent these improvements add an increment of value to our homes, they too may be a variety of *forced* savings.

Good real estate investments require a fair amount of both expertise and time, neither of which is readily available to the small investor. In addition, many require a constant investment of money, if only for taxes. Some accounting-minded investors are bothered by the fact that real estate investments frequently cannot be valued precisely. To others, the lack of precision is a comfort. Certainly, liquidity can be a problem. I am a good example of some of the problems. I live on a farm, which I foremost regard as home, so I am likely never to sell it and realize its underlying value or the profit on its appreciation. Something is always going wrong, so it requires a constant infusion of capital for upkeep. The farm has a fair amount of surplus land, which in theory could be sold as one or more lots, but it requires too much work to keep clear—let alone make attractive to a buyer. I suspect the appreciation, assuming there is some, will be realized by the grandbrats at the very first moment they are in a position to liquidate.

COMMON STOCKS

The third way to acquire ownership—buying common stocks—is more central to the theme of this book than those mentioned above. It also is one subject about which I am supposed to know something. Therefore, I will defer my comments for a later chapter (chapter 14).

When I am talking to college students, I describe these three means of ownership. Then I frequently take a survey and ask the class which of these avenues of investment they would select if I were to give each of them $100,000 and a choice of only one type of ownership. Interestingly enough, the class always selects whichever of the three ownership approaches has performed the best in the previous year or so. If common stocks happen to be bubbling at the moment, they will look at me as if I had asked a really stupid question, considering my occupation. My own answer is that I would select the one that best suited my personal long-term needs and the one in which my financial adviser or I had the most expertise.

•

Some Things Don't Change...

We're ten years later. I've learned quite a few new ways to spend money, but no new ways to invest it; we either lend our savings or use them to acquire and own assets. When we lend our money, we normally receive a set rate of return and a finite date in the future when we get our money back.

It might be helpful conceptually if I give you a list of frequent investments that fall in the lending category:

Money market accounts	Junk bonds
Savings accounts	Municipal bonds
Checking accounts	Corporate bonds
CDs	Preferred stocks*
Treasury notes	Mortgage loans
Cash surrender value of	Federal agency bonds
life insurance	

Preferred stock normally does not have a date of maturity, but it does have a set rate of return, and thus acts more like a bond.

Convertible bonds and stocks have both lending and owning elements. This does not make them the best of both worlds.

When we acquire ownership, whether it is a material good, a piece of real estate, or a common stock, we are not promised a set rate of return; we hope it produces a good return, and though we may sell it, no one promises to give us our money back. All the assets on your balance sheet will fall into either the lending or the earning category. Probably all of the liabilities on your balance sheet will be lendings on the part of someone else to you (with set rates of interest and due dates). Bright as you are, do not place a big figure on your personal intellectual property.

What has changed in the last ten years is that we have become much more a nation of owners by buying common stocks and far less a nation of lenders. Ten years, however, is not forever.

CHAPTER 5

Classifying Assets

Stay with me, kids, we are almost home in this accounting and balance sheet business. I am going to complicate it only one more step. I am assuming, of course, that you used that long list of assets and liabilities in chapter 3 to at least get a handle on where you are at the moment and that you have now divided your assets into lendings and ownership.

Now, I think you will agree with me that simply listing all our assets under either lendings or ownings is a little simplistic. Certainly, we can think of lendings that are quite risky, and we can think of ownership investments that are quite conservative. A concept that I find very useful is to divide our balance sheet into four groups, not just two, and to list our assets in a logical fashion based on the *degree of risk to principal*. A four-way breakdown of our assets covers about 95% of us normal investors quite adequately, and basing it on risk to principal allows us to see where we are financially in order to simplify sound decision making.

Take a look at table 5.1, which I regard as the most important visual aid in this opus, and let me tell you how and why I have created it as I have. Incidentally, don't ignore it as we go along because we are going to use this table as we discuss various aspects of investment policy and the ways to get financially healthier and wealthier.

As you can see in table 5.1, I not only divided the balance sheet into lendings and ownership, I also included three groups of owner-

Table 5.1

Financial Balance Sheet or Portfolio Breakdown

Shares	Security Description	Cost	Market Value	Total	%
	LENDINGS				
	Group I				
	Cash			$ 5,000	
	Money Market			40,000	
	Savings Account			25,000	
	Life Insurance Cash Value			15,000	
	Profit-Sharing Account (1/2 in CD and Bonds)			150,000	
$20,000	U.S. Treasury Note 7.4% due 12/1/96	98.50	100	20,000	
$25,000	Penn. State Univ. 6.2%, due 10/15/00	100	95	23,750	
	Thrift Plan Account (Credit Union, CD)			56,250	
	Subtotal:			**335,000**	
	Less: Liabilities—$10,000 (Credit Cards)			– 10,000	
	Bank Loans—$40,000			– 40,000	
	Total			**$ 285,000**	**36%**
	OWNERSHIP				
	Group II				
	Mutual Fund (Conservative Stocks)	$ 10	$ 10	$ 10,000	
	Bell Atlantic	40	50	10,000	
	Total			**$ 20,000**	**2%**

Group III				
700	IBM	$ 60	$100	$ 70,000
1,000	Mobil	35	50	50,000
1,000	Johnson & Johnson	40	60	60,000
1,200	American Home Products	25	50	60,000
1,500	General Electric	40	40	60,000
	Profit-Sharing Account			
	(½ in high-trade growth stocks)			150,000
	Total			**$ 450,000**	**56%**
	Group IV				
500	Legent Corp.	$ 3	$ 20	$ 10,000
800	Waste Management	10	25	20,000
$20,000	ABC Junk Bond 14% due 1/1/2008	100	50	10,000
500	Respironics	12	20	10,000
	Total			**$ 50,000**	**6%**
	Total Financial Balance Sheet			**$ 805,000**	**100%**
	MISCELLANEOUS				
	Personal Residence			$ 180,000
	Less: Mortgage $50,000			– 50,000
	Vacation Home			100,000
	Total			**$ 230,000**
	Total Net Worth			**$1,035,000**

ship, even though all the asset divisions include common stocks. The basic idea, of course, is that each of these four groups of investments in descending order involves more risk and, it is hoped, more reward.

Now, you might correct me right off and ask me why I put your home at the bottom when it certainly is not the riskiest thing you own. I would agree. However, I put the home at the bottom in a separate category called *Miscellaneous* because it generally will not figure prominently in investment decisions other than the question of whether or not we should pay off our mortgage or borrow against the equity. Frankly, my approach is conditioned by the fact that I work with the financial portfolios of my clients, and I am, therefore, interested in the first four categories and not interested in the details of the improvements to the garage. Different people may use various balance sheet formats for their portfolio breakdowns, particularly people who invest heavily in material goods or real estate.

If you sneak a peek over to the right-hand side of table 5.1, you will see that I subtotaled the financial assets and the percentages of total assets within each group (excluding the home and any personal physical assets you might want to put on your balance sheet). For most of us, this portfolio breakdown is the part of the balance sheet we work with in our financial planning.

Let's play with this a little bit more. You will notice that almost all the lendings are categorized as Group I. Everything in Group I has a set maturity and an established interest rate. Cash, for example, if it is in a checking account, has a maturity of any time you want it and, generally, a low interest rate. The money market fund *comes due* every day and changes the interest rate every day. The municipal bond and the U.S. Treasury note that I included in the portfolio come due in 1995 and the year 2000, respectively. Notice also that I included the cash surrender value of the life insurance, not the face amount of the policy. The cash surrender value is the current realizable value. You must die to get the face amount of the policy—not worth it.

I divided the ownership section into three parts: Group II, Group III, and Group IV. This is an arbitrary division on my part, but one that is important and very useful in terms of investment policy, and one with which I think you will agree. You will learn to classify your own investments according to risk, perhaps not by a rigid formula, but by your perception of risk. Remember, the basic aim in setting up this portfolio breakdown as I have is to list the assets in descending order based on the degree of risk to the principal. All common stocks do not have the same degree of risk, and they can be conveniently classified as conservative (such as telephone companies), as high-grade blue-chip or growth stocks (such as Johnson & Johnson), or as more speculative or aggressive growth investments (such as Legent). You might say, Well, what about a very, very speculative stock or a so-called penny stock? I would agree that it should be listed in your portfolio breakdown. Therefore, you could add Groups V and VI and get down to a lottery ticket in Group VII or Group VIII. The reason I contend that four groups are probably enough is that after Group IV you are not doing aggressive investing. You are gambling, and the odds are very strong that you will lose. I would further contend that any success you have after Group IV will be largely a matter of good luck.

This four-way breakdown of assets allows me to work toward an allocation of assets for virtually all my clients. Notice that I computed a subtotal for Groups I through IV, and I calculated my percentage relationships in the portfolio based on the financial assets. This system allows me to use the groups above Miscellaneous in this balance sheet as a financial planning tool or a financial portfolio breakdown with which I can plan and work more readily. Therefore, if you have material goods that you definitely want to include in your own personal balance sheet, I certainly do not object. I just suggest that you put them down under the Miscellaneous section, so we can work with the financial assets.

With each of these four groups, I have an investment strategy, and I am, therefore, able to characterize the assets that I place in each group.

GROUP I—LENDINGS

My aim in this section of the portfolio is, above all, to protect my principal. Therefore, I want as little volatility in this section as possible, with a secondary aim of producing a reasonable income. This section invariably consists entirely of cash, cash equivalents, and debt securities. Theoretically, we could have an ownership investment in this category, but, in reality, I cannot think of any common stocks that are so stable that I would classify them in the group. Further, although I would include most lendings and debt securities in this group, I can think of plenty of bonds that are not stable enough to include in Group I. For example, if you look at table 5.1, you will notice that I included a junk bond, on which the investor has a pretty good loss, as part of Group IV, on the theory that it has become a very speculative holding. Or I might buy a decent bond with a long maturity, with the aim of producing a profit on the bond from a decline in interest rates, and I would include it in Group II or Group III. As another example, in a period of high interest rates, I might buy a 30-year bond in a good telephone company, which is selling well below par because of high interest rates. I would be buying it to produce a profit by having interest rates decline and my bond move upward toward par. I would not include this bond in Group I because its price volatility will be greater than my requirements for Group I. My aim would be to have the bond appreciate, not to have the price stay the same.

GROUP II—CONSERVATIVE STOCKS

In my view, a Group II security is generally a very high-grade conservative common stock. It is ownership in a business that is basically defensive in nature. We expect the price fluctuations to be considerably less than the fluctuations in the Standard & Poor's Indexes or the Dow Jones Averages—utilities, for example. A few years ago, I felt that many of our better food companies and banks fit into this Group II category. Many of these companies were selling at about seven times earnings and yielding 7%. Then food companies began to grow faster, appreciating in price substantially, and began selling at much higher price-earnings (P-E) ratios. The P-E ratio compares the market price for the stock with the earnings per share of the company. At the moment, therefore, these stocks are not as defensive as they used to be, and I would drop most of the better-known food companies down to Group III. On the other hand, banks began to take very substantial risks, many of which did not work out very well. Their write-offs have increased, their earnings have suffered, and at the moment we might drop a lot of banks all the way down to Group IV.

Aside from the point that Group II stocks are intended to be conservative, remember that a company you buy at one point may move into another group because of either its price action or the company's performance. A good food stock at 7 times earnings is a lot more conservative than a good food stock at 16 times earnings. If either price or business conditions change the basic nature of the investment, you change the ranking you have given it in your balance sheet.

GROUP III—HIGH-GRADE COMMON STOCKS

The aim of Group III investments might be characterized as a *balanced offense.* We are no longer primarily concerned with protecting our principal. Our goal is to produce profits in a reasonable and measured fashion.

Group III generally consists of high-grade growth stocks and blue-chip companies. You will recognize the names in our model portfolio. They are not conservative enough to be Group II stocks, and they are certainly not as aggressive as Group IV stocks. Yet, if a smaller company is very strong financially, and has a steady earnings record as well as an excellent position in its industry, I include it in Group III.

Note that in this particular model portfolio, the family has a substantial investment in a profit-sharing plan. In classifying this plan, I studied the holdings of the plan just enough to realize that about half the money was invested in high-grade debt securities and the other half in high-grade common stocks. Therefore, I split the profit-sharing plan in two. You will see $150,000 under Group I representing the lendings, and $150,000 in Group III representing the high-grade stocks.

Most real estate and material goods investments fall into Group III or Group IV. It is certainly possible to have a real estate investment that has the quality of a Group II common stock, but I cannot think of any that would be descriptive to you. We could, however, visualize many real estate transactions that are very blue chip in nature and merit a Group III rating.

GROUP IV—AGGRESSIVE-GROWTH STOCKS

The objective of Group IV investments is almost exclusively appreciation in value. This group generally consists of smaller companies, considered by many to be more speculative investments. Since our classifications are done by risk to principal, we could very well have a sizable company in Group IV simply because this particular company's stock does not merit inclusion in the higher-quality groups of the portfolio. Examples are major industrial companies or banks that hit very difficult times and, therefore, became more speculative. Owning Chrysler is a lot different from owning General Electric.

Most material goods probably belong in this section. Think of the price action of even a van Gogh over a period of time, and you could regard it as a very valuable but speculative investment.

These divisions are certainly debatable. Nobody tells you when you buy a stock precisely where it fits and that it should be classified as a Group II, III, or IV. Some years ago a mechanism called *beta* was developed, which measures historical stock fluctuations with the intention of giving investors some idea as to whether their stock moves slower or faster than, or about the same as, the stock market as a whole. The stock market presumably has a beta of 1.0. Thus, faster-moving stocks have betas in excess of 1.0 and slower-moving stocks have betas less than 1.0, for example, .6. A company with a high beta normally fits in Group IV, and a company with a very low beta normally fits in Group II or Group III. Keep in mind, the beta measurement does not tell you how this company will perform in the future; it simply gives an indication of what might be expected in the near future as to the movement of the price of the company's stock.

As we move down from Group I through Group IV, we can see that we are generally increasing our risk and, it is hoped, our rewards. This risk/reward relationship is basic to investing. There is no rule that says you will receive greater rewards by assuming greater risk, but at least we can get the idea that we are looking for greater rewards. Presumably, if we are operating well, our Group I's will sit quietly and do nothing but produce a reasonable income. Group II's should be relatively quiet, particularly in down markets. It is a delight when a Group II stock becomes a Group III over a period of time by showing that it can increase its earnings and become more of a growth stock (e.g., food companies). It is also nice when your original investment in a Group IV stock is justified by consistent growth in earnings and stature, which leads you to consider moving the stock from Group IV into Group III. The concept is simply that the fortunes of a company and its stock do change over a period of time, and the basic nature of an individual investment, therefore, changes sometimes for the better and sometimes for the worse.

It is not very important to debate the group into which a particular company should be classified, but it is important to do your balance sheet with this four-way portfolio breakdown in mind and determine what percentage of your assets are in each group. Needless to say, kids, we will come back to these percentage relationships.

•

I'm Back Already in 2001 . . .

This is a very important chapter for your investment policy, and it is a bit demanding, so let me just summarize what we are trying to do:

1. We have previously made a list of all our assets and liabilities, and we divided our assets into lendings and ownership. If these assets were in fact bigger than our debts, our net worth (wealth) could be calculated simply by subtracting our liabilities from our assets. Worth remembering. If our debts are more than our Group I holdings, we are essentially borrowing to hold our ownership assets. If our assets are less than our liabilities or lifestyle, we are technically broke.

2. Now we complicate our efforts a little bit, to give ourselves a clear approach for our investment policy. We put our lending assets in Group I. We complicate our ownership assets by dividing them into three groups based on our judgment of perceived risk to principal in the asset. You'll get a feel for these from table 5.1. It divides our ownership assets into Groups II, III, and IV.

This business of classifying our investments into the four groups can sometimes require a difficult judgment. Mutual funds are a good example. Ten years ago, in table 5.1 I divided a conservative balanced mutual fund into its bond component (Group I) and its stock component (Group III). At the same time, I would have upgraded a diversified stock portfolio by a group to recognize the moderating influence of diversification.

I'm far less inclined to upgrade most mutual funds today because of the high market, the higher turnover rate in so many funds, and fund managers' increased interest in short-term results. Today a fund with a bunch of Group IV stocks I'd consider a Group IV investment, not a Group III investment.

Let's make two other minor changes from our list of assets/liabilities:

1. We look at our liabilities against Group I. Our liabilities are an absolute claim against all of our assets, and we are simply applying our borrowings to our lendings; this allows us to compute percentages of our net financial assets in each of the four groups (see table 5.1). After we've balanced our debts against our lendings (Group I).
2. My personal exception or forgiveness on debts is our home mortgage. Our home is where we live, but unless we plan to sell it, it's usually not a vital ingredient in our financial investment policy.
3. At this point we can compute the percentages of our financial assets in each of the four groups, as you can see in table 5.1.

Big step, kids. These percentages are the foundation for what is going to be our unique policy. Stay with me. If you are not clear, then spend a little bit more time with table 5.1 before you nod off. Think about each of your assets and where they fit. Compute your percentages and begin to get an impression of how conservative or aggressive you are. If you've done this really well, I'll let you skip the next two chapters.

I remember a cartoon in *The New Yorker* of two little boys after the crash of '87, one saying to the other, "I got through it pretty well. All my assets were in baseball cards." Group IV.

CHAPTER 6

Pay Your Debts

YOU KIDS JUST KNEW THAT AT SOME POINT YOU WERE GOING to have to listen to a five-minute lecture on paying your debts, otherwise known as eliminating your liabilities. You knew it, you just *knew* it! Five minutes seems reasonable to me.

The first thing to remember about any debts you have is that they are an absolute claim or obligation against everything you own. To illustrate this concept, I want you to review table 5.1 and find the liabilities section. You will notice that I put two of the debts in Group I as deductions from the assets in that group. I do not care whether you incur the debt to buy a car, fix up the front porch, or take a well-deserved vacation. If you owe the money, the obligation is as strong for you to pay your debts as it is for the U.S. Treasury to pay its debts. Therefore, you should show your debts against the highest-ranking assets you have—your lendings in Group I. If I put my debts right up there at the top of my balance sheet against my most stable assets, I see them pretty quickly when I do my balance sheet, and it makes me think about them.

Thus, looking right square and smart at our liabilities near the top of our balance sheet every six months leads us very quickly to the consideration of paying the debt as an economic trade-off. This is the second concept I would like to have you consider relative to your debts. To my lender, I, as the borrower, may be anything from a good risk to a junk-bond risk, but I am certainly not as good as the U.S. Treasury, which can always print money. My creditor will, therefore, charge me for the degree of risk that he thinks I deserve.

He is also going to charge me for all the paperwork and time to make me the loan. He may even like me, but he is lending to me to make money. If I keep my liabilities right up at the top of my balance sheet, I can recognize the trade-offs that exist for me in terms of what I get for lending my money and what I pay for borrowing it. If the rate of interest on a debt is greater than that which you earn on a cash investment, such as a money market, there is no question you are better off paying off the debt. If, for example, you have a large credit card balance at 17% interest—a common rate—and your money market is only earning 8%, pay off the balance. You will be far ahead. In table 5.1, for example, I suggest that this family think of using a chunk of their money market fund to pay off a corresponding chunk of their liabilities. There may be some unique reason for not doing so, but all across the United States people borrow chunks of money at the same time they lend money, and the *spread* is generally against them.

I am willing to compromise on home mortgage debt simply because, as I said, most Americans cannot afford to buy homes outright, and, as I already inferred, I am generally in favor of home ownership. In table 5.1, you can see that I put the home mortgage liability against the home at the bottom of the balance sheet. Congress implies they share my view by allowing us to deduct the interest on our home mortgage but not on our consumer installment debts. Well, maybe they do not share this view, but they sure know that there are millions of noisy Americans with home mortgages who are already mad at Congress. At least they are smart enough to know they do not need a whole group of voters who are even madder.

Relative to your debts, the least you can do is to do your math. A couple of very simple math exercises are applicable primarily to you young kids, who have a reputation of being the instant-gratification generation. I have seen a lot of sizable purchases that might not be characterized as necessities made with borrowed money, sometimes because they "really got a bargain." As you are getting the bargain, you might sit down for a moment and add all the interest you will pay while you are enjoying the bargain, and you may come to the conclusion that you have a fairly expensive gratification.

By now, you have correctly inferred that I am pretty dead set against liabilities and believe it is generally an excellent investment to pay them off. In fairness, I should say that this is one of those points on which many experts and I disagree, and they have a case. I have heard many smart kids say that the way to become successful and wealthy is to borrow as much money as you can and produce an inordinate rate of return on these borrowings. They point out that this country is such a nation of lenders (and borrowers) that we really are not charged enough for our borrowings. Conversely, of course, we do not get enough interest on our lendings, a point with which I agree. In any event, the prodigious borrower contends that other people's money is cheap to obtain in the United States, a point with which I also agree. The conclusion, however, that we should therefore use other people's money for investing is where we part company.

When I came into the securities business, the vast majority of the clients in our firm used margin accounts. They borrowed money to buy stocks. A few years ago, I did a little study of margin accounts and found that borrowers who were able to buy more stock through leveraging actually did worse in their performance than people who bought less stock and paid cash for it. Assuming this is true, *why* is it true? Well, I attribute it largely to the psychological pressures that come from owing money as well as owning fluctuating stocks. When the stock market is declining precipitously, the person with a margin account feels the pressure of the debt. This pressure will build until he or she takes the loss instead of waiting for the market to go back up. The investor, therefore, has a tendency to sell low. When the market is going up, the margin account investor becomes convinced of the wisdom in borrowing money to buy stocks. He then borrows more money and buys more stock while riding the euphoria of a bull market. He, therefore, has a tendency to buy high. My conclusion is that the psychological pressure of owing money increases the already natural tendency of an individual to buy high and sell low in stock market cycles.

Just as we each have inclinations toward being a spender or a saver, we each have a psychological tolerance for debt, and I think it is worthwhile to consider your own. The concept that people who have sizable debts are uncomfortable with them is not necessarily valid. Some of us certainly are, but I know plenty of people who have no problem leading their lives with a good slug of debt.

I will describe my own psychological makeup, not because it's perfect, but as a framework for evaluating yourself. As an investor, I incur a good bit of risk, measured risk I hope. Occasionally, I borrow a chunk of money when I find I want to make an investment that must be done promptly, and I do not want to sell something immediately to make this investment. Once I incur the debt, I am very conscious of it. Yes, I know I can equate it to the investment I made using the borrowed money, but I also know it is an obligation against everything I have. Therefore, I have a tendency to pay off this debt a lot faster than is necessary. As a risk-taking investor, it allows me to tell myself that I really own this stock. It may go from $50 to $5, but I own it and nobody is going to tell me I have to sell it. I find this is an enormous comfort in down markets, and it permits me the mental freedom to make aggressive investments at points when the stock market is indicating that the world is about to end, which it usually does not. It also allows me to do one thing in this world that I am very good at and enjoy thoroughly—sleep.

Now, let me contrast this approach with that of a person who advocates a judicious use of debt. This person believes in himself and his security selection enough to risk more than his own money on the investment. This does not mean that he is financially unstable. Certainly, he can live with it psychologically and may sleep even better than I do, although that is unlikely. His contention is that he makes substantially better returns from his investment than I do. During pleasant periods in the stock market, he is right; he does produce more appreciation. If he is well-disciplined, he can certainly use the debt to augment his performance and pay it down as his stocks appreciate. However, my approach makes me look better on the downside, and my claim is that I can, as a product of my approach, be an aggressive buyer at very low points in the market and make up for his better performance during the good periods. With his debt as a burden, he cannot be an aggressive purchaser in bad periods because he does not have the financial capability at that point to do so. This is the kind of debate that could last all night. The important question is, What kind of person are you?

Understanding what kind of attitude you have toward debt is very important. Whatever your attitude, do your math. Look at the trade-offs. However, if you are a good spender, have a high tolerance for debt and a skinny balance sheet, you must be a whale of a good sleeper!

•

Ten Years Later...

As soon as I finished writing this chapter on the wisdom of paying your debts, Americans immediately stopped paying their debts and began incurring constantly and consistently higher levels of debt. This was aided primarily by the fact that we Americans now learn to use a credit card before we learn to write a check.

All of us in the financial world worry about an impending consumer debt problem, but no widespread catastrophe has yet occurred. We do have a constantly increasing number of personal bankruptcies. Oddly enough, the major chunk of this debt, incurred by young people, stems from a very wise use of their borrowed money in the form of college education. In a way, we are doing a wonderful thing in educating barrels of kids, but at the same time we are teaching them that they can live with enormous levels of debt.

I'd certainly stress the ability to understand your own tolerance for debt and the correlation with your own happiness. Most of my time is spent with people who have money and want to invest it well, but I have seen a few cases where people, even though they have jobs, have basically lost their freedom because of debts. That's sad.

Worth repeating is the desirability of correlating your money management with your happiness.

CHAPTER 7

Advanced Accounting

You ARE DOING GREAT, KIDS. I PROMISED THAT IF YOU DID your balance sheet, I would let you go outdoors and play. Therefore, if you know very well you are not going to do any more accounting than we have already done, this chapter, which explains profit and loss (P&L) statements and how to create budgets, is optional reading and you can skip to chapter 8. This chapter is suggested reading for those who feel this record-keeping subject is worth a couple of hours a month and not just every six months. However, if you are among those who have real trouble living within your income and do not already have a very good system, it is required reading.

Our P&L statement is the record that tells us how we are doing financially as we go merrily along between balance sheets. An analogy to illustrate the difference between the two might be that a balance sheet is the box score at the end of the game, and the P&L statement is a video of the game itself. The P&L statement, a record of income and expenses, tells us each month whether we are operating profitably or losing money. As I mentioned, the changes in our balance sheets from one period to another will reflect how we are doing, so we can come pretty close to measuring profitability from our balance sheets. It could well be, however, that our investments are appreciating at the same time we are operating in the red, so our lack of profitability can be disguised on our balance sheets by the appreciation of our assets. The reverse is also true. So your P&L

statement, which gives you a truer picture of how you are operating, can be very important to understanding your financial fitness.

Savers are far more inclined to keep track of their income and expenses than *spenders*. Some years ago, a lady came to see me and told me she had $1,000 to invest. Her husband was a very successful doctor and had been for a number of years. When we got into the question of the family's financial balance sheet, however, it turned out that she was exactly right; she merely had $1,000 to invest. Her husband had probably earned at least $1 million in the previous ten years, and they had spent $999,000 of that $1 million. Our association ended when I concluded a brief lecture with the observation that with a little effort they could probably find something on which they could spend the last $1,000.

Moreover, some small percentage of people actually *like* keeping records. Grown-up kids who liked baseball when they were younger kids frequently are better at P&Ls than most people, because statistics are part of the lifeblood of the true baseball fan. Some kids, of course, never convert from baseball records to income and expense records. Keeping P&Ls through the new software available today is great exercise for computer kids.

If we can learn so much from our balance sheet, why should we keep records of our income and expenses? Well, for those who file complicated tax returns, such records are far better than throwing your slips in a drawer. The better answer, however, is the fact that when we keep track of expenses, the records have some impact psychologically on how we spend money. I strongly suggest income and expense records for young people on tight budgets. Many people feel they are being very careful with their money when, in fact, they are frittering away small amounts they would save if they knew how much they frittered every month. As reinforcement for the importance of saving even small amounts over time, take another look at tables 2.2 and 2.5 to remind yourself how rich you can be if you save a little and compound successfully. This is not meant to be a lecture because I fritter, too. The fact remains, however, that keeping track of income and expenses will have a favorable impact on most of us that may not even be perceptible while it is occurring.

Keeping track of our income and expenses is not as difficult a task as it appears to be before we actually do it. You can buy little record books in most good stationery or business-supply stores. Most of these are designed with large numbers of people in mind, but not with you specifically in mind. If you look at a few models, however, you may find one that fits you nicely. However, making up your own is not very difficult. You may have to experiment with it for a month or two to set up the system that works best for you, but if you get into the habit, you will find it rather easy.

To help you set up your own personalized income and expense form, take a look at table 7.1, an enormous list of income and expense items, many of which you will, I hope, never incur. Don't be frightened. Just scratch out all the items that do not pertain to you, or lump them together so that you can put them under one heading. For example, lump Gas, Electric, and Water/sewer all under the heading of Utilities. The aim is to come down to a manageable number of categories for all your expenses.

Now, take a squint at table 7.2, which uses nothing more than a columnar pad, to design your own income and expense form. For clarity, I have broken it into two parts for this book. After wasting a couple of sheets during experimentation, you can probably design one of these for each month, customize it with your own expense categories from table 7.1, and it will suit you perfectly.

For most of us, our income items are not very numerous, and we can simply list our income each month from various sources. I put this at the lower-left section of the monthly ledger in table 7.2.

Our expenses, however, generally fall into two categories:

1. Those we incur monthly, which require only one payment per month. You can see some of these on the lower-right side of the monthly ledger. One figure a month will generally do it.
2. Those we incur sporadically or even daily during the month. That is why we need the columns with our own particular headings in the daily-expense ledger. Fill in the amounts each day as you incur these expenses.

Table 7.1

List of Monthly Income and Expenses

	Income
1	Salary
2	Salary—spouse
3	Child support
4	Alimony
5	Dividend income
6	Interest income
7	Notes/loans receivable
8	Mortgages receivable
9	Trust income
10	Pension income
11	Other income
	Total Income

	Expenses
1	Moving expenses
2	Employee business expense
3	IRA
4	IRA—spouse
5	KEOGH
6	KEOGH—spouse
7	Interest penalties
8	Alimony payments
9	Federal income tax
10	State income tax
11	Local income tax

Table 7.1 *(continued)*

List of Monthly Income and Expenses

12	Other withholdings
13	Social security
14	Property tax
15	Charitable contributions
16	Union dues
17	Financial services
18	Bank charges
19	Rent
20	Mortgage principal
21	Mortgage interest
22	Second home principal
23	Second home interest
24	Other interest
25	Homeowner's insurance
26	Auto insurance
27	Health insurance
28	Life insurance
29	Disability insurance
30	Liability insurance
31	Other insurance
32	Home repair
33	Auto repair
34	Auto expense
35	Licenses
36	Auto loans
37	Other loans
38	Charge cards

Table 7.1 *(continued)*

List of Monthly Income and Expenses

	Expenses *(continued)*
39	Savings
40	Investments
41	Child support
42	Child care
43	Care for other dependents
44	Domestic help
45	Doctors
46	Dentists
47	Medical—prescriptions
48	Medical—other
49	Electricity
50	Gas
51	Water/sewer
52	Trash removal
53	Miscellaneous utilities
54	Telephone
55	Gifts
56	Food—at home
57	Food—out
58	Clothing
59	Cleaning/laundry
60	Personal care
61	Pet care
62	Entertainment
63	Vacations
64	Hobbies/recreation

Table 7.1 *(continued)*
List of Monthly Income and Expenses

65	Books/magazines/newspapers	
66	Education	
67	Allowances	
68	Appliances	
	Total Expenses	

At the end of each month, you can give your adding machine about a 15-minute workout to determine whether you are profitable or unprofitable for the month. If you are unprofitable every month and do not have a fat balance sheet, you can at least infer that you have a problem and maybe have a pretty good idea what the size of your problem is.

After you finish your income and expense sheet each month, I suggest you spend two more minutes simply thinking about your income versus your expenses. For people who have never done this exercise, this appears to be a lot of work, and one of questionable merit. My contention is, however, that the total time and devotion to this activity will be about five minutes a day and that if you allow it to become a habit, it will become both painless and rewarding. If you are one of those people who spends small amounts daily, for candy bars, newspapers, etc., then simply estimate these things at $1 to $2 per day and put it on your P&L this way—so you do not have to keep track of every dime.

There is one final step worth mentioning to those many individuals who have a tight financial situation or to those few individuals who happen to enjoy record keeping. I recommend that you take the next accounting step beyond the income and expense level: Create a budget. It is prudent of me to recommend it, but frankly, I am not about to do it myself. I will confess to you

Table 7.2
Income and Expense Worksheet

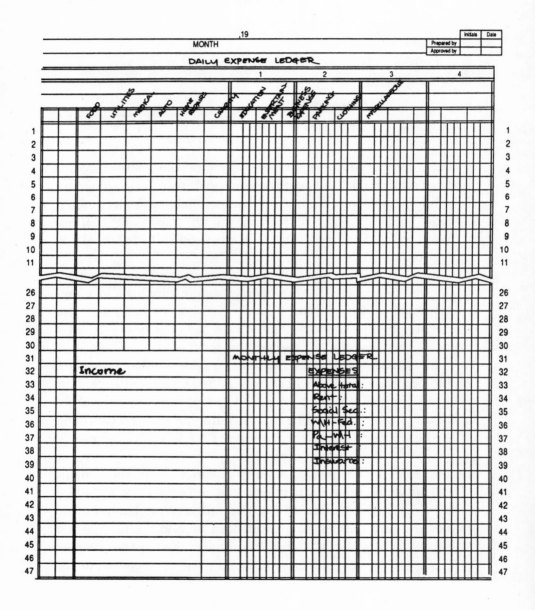

that, aside from having some awareness of future sizable expenditures, I have just never been able to put up with the fuss of doing a detailed budget. I support and admire those who receive the psychological and financial benefits that flow from budgeting and living by the budget. If this seems to be a strange attitude from a financial adviser, I further confess that although I characterize my clients/friends as *spenders* or *savers*, I avoid intruding very far into their P&L statements unless they ask for some guidance. I am supposed to make sure the balance sheet is invested well, not take away the joys of *frittering* money. That part is up to you.

·

The Easy Way Out...

If you have absolutely no intention of keeping track of your expenses, I'll apologize for including chapter 7. Needless to say, it is rather desirable, especially for young people, to have a good understanding of the relationship between your income and your expenses. Why don't we therefore pretend that chapter 7 is for that small percentage of us who don't mind a bit of time and effort to have a good overview of how we're doing financially in our day-to-day living.

There are easier ways than this to get a feeling of your profitability. If your checking account is going down and your debit balances are going up, you have a pretty good clue. If you do your balance sheet as promised every six months and compare them as you go, you will know how you're doing. For this we'll give you a passing grade. Most Americans flunk.

CHAPTER 8

Great Expectations

LISTEN UP, KIDS; THIS CHAPTER IS IMPORTANT. AS YOU WILL recall, my opening sentence in this opus was: "The essence of an investment policy is to relate the situation of the investor to the world in which we live." Well, "the world in which we live" is full of inflation. To combat its effects, investors can employ stocks and bonds and other vehicles to invest their money. I hope this chapter will give you a better understanding of what you can expect from your investments and how you might set your investment goals.

My impression of the average American's viewpoint on inflation, bonds, and stocks is this: Inflation is always with us and gradually erodes the purchasing power of our savings; bonds are generally good, safe investments for producing income but not very satisfactory in fighting inflation; stocks, over a period of time, may be better investments than bonds, but they are certainly risky. Now, these impressions are fine as far as they go, but I want you to have a somewhat deeper understanding of each and how they might interrelate as you develop your all-season investment policy.

To have a little fun, we will pretend you are in a contest. Your entry blank, which must be turned in tomorrow, reads as follows:

Mrs. Greatworth is leaving the country for a round-the-world vacation that will last exactly ten years. She wants you, and several other contestants, to invest $100,000 for her while she is gone. She is an extremely conservative investor who abhors risk and simply wants to maintain the purchasing power she already has—and Mrs. Greatworth has so much money already that she does not need her investments to appreciate faster than inflation. If you make too much money, you lose. You have taken too much risk. In this contest, any income produced by your investment will be spent, and no taxes apply, so your sole objective is to ensure that the principal keeps pace with the purchasing power changes over the next ten years, as measured by the consumer price index (CPI). Whoever comes closest at the end of ten years to matching the original purchasing power of Mrs. Greatworth's $100,000 wins the contest. Your entry must be filed tomorrow.

How would you invest the $100,000?

We will pretend it is a good prize, let's say $1 million. Mrs. Greatworth and I will settle for a general answer. Make a tentative answer now.

Let's think of some of the factors that we might consider before we finalize your entry blank. I will raise some questions and you give your answers as we go. Then, I will add a little bit of history and perhaps some logic to each question and give you my answer. If you want to keep this book ten years, you can drop me a note and tell me how wrong I was.

Question One: What will the average inflation rate be over the next ten years?

Write your guess in this blank: _____%

If history would help you with this guess, go back to table 2.3 (page 30). In the third column, you will see the annual cost of living increase each year since 1939. You will notice there were only three years, none since 1954, in which the cost of living *decreased*. There were also only three years in which inflation hit double-digit figures. In the last three or four years, it's been in the 4 1/2% range. Slide your eye over to the last column on table 2.3 and note the ten-year average rate for the previous decade, which might narrow your guess a bit. It may also make you yearn for those good old days in the late 1950s and early 1960s when the average rate was under 2%.

In this contest, you are allowed to apply political studies, economic models, tea leaves, or whatever you like to arrive at your inflation forecast. I will keep my studies simple, since this is a ten-year period and I am still planning next week. My guess is that we are just finishing a period of lower-than-normal inflation. We have had an ample supply of most basic commodities, such as oil, and generally enjoyed a period of peace, which certainly does not cost as much as war. On the other hand, we are now faced with the problems of paying for an enormous level of debt, including the necessity of bailing out the S&Ls and maybe even a bunch of banks. I would be somewhat more optimistic about inflation if I could see any signs that Congress intends to become more responsible in handling the nation's budget and tax questions. Since this opus is not an economics textbook, however, I just guess 5.9% annually for the 1990s and hope that my guess is high.

Question Two: **Based on your inflation guess, how much will the $100,000 have to appreciate to have the same purchasing power in ten years?**

My guess is I will have to end up with $_____ to hold the purchasing power.

You can compute this answer exactly, but I know you won't. Therefore, you can do a little practice with the rule of 72 and come pretty close. If you guess 7.2% on inflation, you can divide that into the magic number 72 and conclude that you must precisely double the $100,000 in ten years to win the contest. A second way is to find the ten-year average rate of inflation in table 2.3 that comes closest to your guess and then move one column to the left. It will show you by what percentage you must increase the $100,000 to win the contest. For example, if your guess is 6.6% for inflation, you will note that that is the rate for the decade ending in 1986, and the column to the left shows you would have to increase the principal by 90%—to $190,000—to hit your figure.

I've been teasing you. There is a very simple way to translate your inflation expectation into a dollar figure ten years hence. Just go back to table 2.5 (page 36), which shows $10,000 compounded at different rates over ten years. Add a zero to the figure you see, and you will know precisely the amount of your target. Pause for a moment and consider your guess on inflation and the ramifications for your investment policy. Unless your inflation guess is very low, *you will be forced to take risks to protect the purchasing power of your savings.* The faster the rate of inflation, the more risk you have to take. Clearly, inflation presents you with a severe challenge in investing your savings.

Question Three: **What rate of appreciation do you expect from your lendings (your fixed income investments)?**

I expect my lendings to appreciate at ___% annually.

Remember, don't count interest income. Mrs. Greatworth is spending all her income—we set that rule for the contest. Your primary lending vehicles, savings accounts and bonds, are contracts in which the borrower promises to repay your principal, not your purchasing power.

If your guess on inflation in the 1990s was anywhere close to mine, I suspect your answer to this question should be zero; no appreciation from bonds. If your guess on inflation was very low, you could probably aim for some appreciation by buying very long-term bonds and figuring that interest rates will decline as inflation declines, thereby giving you a bit of appreciation on your bonds.

One thing we learned from the 1980s is that buying bonds can be a very risky enterprise. There are plenty of investors across the country, including financial institutions, who wish today that their net change in principal on their lending activities for the 1980s had been zero.

A few of you will think of a sneaky way to win the contest by buying a ten-year zero % coupon bond with a yield to maturity roughly identical to your guess on the inflation rate. In case you are not familiar with *zeros*, they are bonds that pay no interest but are sold, both originally and subsequently, at a discount to their face value. Owners make their *interest* through the appreciation that occurs from the point of purchase until the maturity date. This investment might be the most conservative way to try to win the contest, but Mrs. Greatworth might be a little unhappy with you for producing no income and having her pay taxes over the years.

Personally, this lending question is the one I can answer with certainty. My target in terms of capital appreciation from my fixed income investments will be zero, and that is exactly what I expect to produce. I will buy ten-year bonds at par and have them come due the day the contest ends, with no gain or loss. (Preferably, *I* would buy five-year bonds twice during the contest.)

You will note by now that this investing game is getting tougher. If our inflation guess is 5% or 6%, and we have to produce appreciation of $60,000 to $80,000, and we probably cannot get any of it by lending our money, it becomes a pretty tough game. Therefore, we have to take risks, we have to become owners, if we are going to fight inflation successfully.

Question Four: **What ownership investments do you want to make?**

I plan to invest in the ownership of _____ stocks and/or _____ real estate and/or _____ material goods.

I do not want to inhibit you in any way from winning the prize, so if you have a favorite alternative that will produce the appreciation we need, you are all set.

Back to history for context. Turn to table 8.1, which shows the investment performance of various alternatives over the last 20-, 10-, 5-, and 1-year periods. Note that it is for the period ending June 1, 1991. Also note that these returns include dividend and interest income, so you must adjust stocks down 3% or 4% for dividends, bonds down 7% or 8% for interest, and wipe out the return on U.S. Treasury bills.

Table 8.1 surprises me a bit. House prices seem to be about as close as any of the alternatives in staying near the inflation rate shown at the bottom of the chart. If we bought a $100,000 house, however, once again the sponsor might get a little upset because she received no income and has had to pay annual real estate taxes. Farmland also disappointed me by being no better than the inflation rate for the 20-year period and considerably worse in shorter periods. Much as I love them, those amber waves of grain have not done much for a decade.

Some material goods investment may appreciate greatly in the 1990s, but most of us better stick with stocks, even after deducting dividends, because their performance is more reliable. I don't think I want to buy an old master painting, and I am not sure I would know a Chinese ceramic if I saw one.

Question Five: **What appreciation, if any, will occur in the Dow Jones Industrial Average (DJIA) or the Standard & Poor's 500 Stock Index (S&P 500) through the 1990s?**

I guess that the total appreciation of the DJIA or the S&P 500 will be ___ % in the 1990s.

To me, this is the toughest question in the contest unless you happen to be a whiz at some kind of material goods investing and, therefore, do not have to answer it. The likelihood of continued inflation, the inability of lendings to hedge it, and our material goods constraints together would force most of us to agree that we have to assume some risk through common stock investing in order to win the contest.

Take a look at table 8.2, the DJIA over the last 65 years, and table 8.3, the S&P 500 over the last 65 years. Spend a few minutes with them. We don't have to get our entry form in until tomorrow, so study the tables to give yourself a concept of history. Although you may be fascinated with these tables, keep in mind what we are

Table 8.1
The Asset Derby

Asset Category	Investment Performance[1]			
	20 Years	10 Years	5 Years	1 Year
Old master paintings	12.3%	15.8%	23.4%	6.5%
Stocks	11.6	16.0	13.3	11.8
Chinese ceramics	11.6	8.1	15.1	3.6
Gold	11.5	– 2.9	1.0	– 0.7
Diamonds	10.5	6.4	10.2	0.0
Stamps	10.0	– 0.7	– 2.4	– 7.7
Bonds	9.4	15.2	9.7	13.2
Oil	8.9	– 5.9	8.5	20.7
Treasury bills (3-month)	8.6	8.8	7.0	7.1
House prices	7.3	4.4	4.6	4.7
Farmland (U.S.)	6.3	– 1.8	1.3	2.1
Silver	5.0	– 9.3	– 4.8	–18.9
Foreign exchange	4.5	3.8	5.4	0.2
Consumer Price Index	**6.3%**	**4.3%**	**4.5%**	**5.0%**

[1]Compound annual return (including dividend or interest income, if any) for periods ended June 1, 1991.
Source: Salomon Bros.

trying to do: get a feel for the historical movement in high-grade stock prices over an extended period of time and where we are at the beginning of 1991. Then, relate these historical results to the challenge of inflation.

Some would contend, not without reason, that the DJIA, with only 30 stocks, is not broad enough to be a truly good stock market indicator. Furthermore, it is not immutable. In the 25 years from 1964 through 1989, there is some contrast between those stocks that were dropped from the DJIA and those that were added (see page 90).

Would you not agree that the DJIA gets upgraded over a period of time by its change in composition?

I will make my observations on the S&P 500 (table 8.3), since it is a bit broader with 500 stocks. This table is loaded with historical stock market information, and you will be able to form some useful impressions.

Let's first take a look at a long period of time, from 1926 to 1990. At the bottom, you will notice that the consumer price increase was 647%, while earnings and dividends increased over 1,600%. That is encouraging. Year-end prices increased even more—2,498%. Inflation was bad, but earnings and dividends substantially more than made up for it, and stock prices did even better. At the bottom of the table, you can see that over the 65-year period the compound annual rate of return of the S&P 500 was 10%, a conclusion that is in the same ballpark as most other long-term studies of stock prices. For our purposes, we can at least agree that it has not been necessary to have anything like 100% of our assets in common stocks to fight inflation.

To keep you on table 8.3, we might take a little closer look at the last ten years, a period in which the S&P 500 increased almost two and one-half times, from 135 at the end of 1980 to 330 at the end of 1990. This was a great period for common stock investors, since the inflation rate dropped off substantially during the 1980s. Let's go a little deeper. The dividend rate almost doubled during the 1980s, but dividends presumably come from earnings, and earnings

Table 8.2
Dow Jones Industrial Average 65-Year Performance (1926–1990)

| Year | Market | | | | Earnings | Dividends | Annual Total Return | Year-End Yield | Year-End P-E Multiple | Book Value | Consumer Price Index 1982–84 = 100 |
	High	Low	Close	Annual Change							
1925	—	—	156.66	—	—	—	—	—	—	—	17.9
1926	166.64	135.20	157.20	0.3	11.39	5.54	3.9	3.51	13.8	75.2	17.7
1927	202.40	152.73	202.40	28.8	8.72	6.04	32.6	2.98	23.2	77.9	17.3
1928	300.00	191.33	300.00	48.2	15.97	9.76	53.0	3.25	18.8	84.1	17.1
1929	381.17	198.69	248.48	-17.2	19.94	12.75	-12.9	5.13	12.5	91.3	17.2
1930	294.04	157.51	164.58	-33.8	11.02	11.13	-29.3	6.76	14.9	91.2	16.1
1931	194.36	73.79	77.90	-52.7	4.09	8.40	-47.6	10.78	19.1	86.9	14.6
1932	88.78	41.22	59.93	-23.1	-.51	4.62	-17.1	7.71	*	81.8	13.1
1933	108.67	50.16	99.90	66.7	2.11	3.40	72.4	3.40	47.4	80.5	13.1
1934	110.74	85.51	104.04	4.1	3.91	3.66	7.8	3.52	26.6	80.7	13.4
1935	148.44	96.71	144.13	38.5	6.34	4.55	42.9	3.16	22.7	82.50	13.8
1936	184.90	143.11	179.90	24.8	10.07	7.05	29.7	3.92	17.9	85.55	14.0
1937	194.40	113.64	120.85	-32.8	11.49	8.78	-27.9	7.27	10.5	88.30	14.4
1938	158.41	98.95	154.76	28.1	6.01	4.98	32.2	3.22	25.8	87.13	14.0
1939	155.92	121.44	150.25	-2.9	9.11	6.11	1.0	4.07	16.5	95.58	13.9
1940	152.80	111.84	131.13	-12.7	10.92	7.06	-8.0	5.38	12.0	98.75	14.1
1941	133.59	106.34	110.96	-15.4	11.64	7.59	-9.6	6.84	9.5	102.33	15.5
1942	119.17	92.92	119.40	7.6	9.22	6.40	13.4	5.36	13.0	107.50	16.9
1943	145.82	119.26	135.89	13.8	9.74	6.30	19.1	4.64	14.0	113.03	17.4
1944	152.53	134.22	152.32	12.1	10.07	6.57	16.9	4.31	15.1	118.33	17.8
1945	195.82	151.35	192.91	26.6	10.56	6.69	31.0	3.47	18.3	122.74	18.2
1946	212.50	163.12	177.20	-8.1	13.63	7.50	-4.3	4.23	13.0	131.40	21.5
1947	186.85	163.21	181.16	2.2	18.80	9.21	7.4	5.08	9.6	149.08	23.4
1948	193.16	165.39	177.30	-2.1	23.07	11.50	4.2	6.49	7.7	159.67	24.1
1949	200.52	161.60	200.13	12.9	23.54	12.79	20.1	6.39	8.5	170.12	23.6
1950	235.47	196.81	235.41	17.6	30.70	16.13	25.7	6.85	7.7	194.19	25.0
1951	276.37	238.99	269.23	14.4	26.59	16.34	21.3	6.07	10.1	202.60	26.5
1952	292.00	256.35	291.90	8.4	24.78	15.48	14.2	5.30	11.8	213.39	26.7
1953	293.79	255.49	289.90	-3.8	27.23	16.11	4.8	5.56	10.7	244.26	26.9
1954	404.39	279.87	404.39	39.5	28.18	17.47	45.5	4.32	14.4	248.96	26.7
1955	488.40	388.20	488.40	20.8	35.78	21.58	26.1	4.41	13.7	271.77	26.8
1956	521.05	462.35	499.47	2.3	33.34	22.99	7.0	4.60	15.0	284.78	27.6
1957	520.77	419.79	435.69	-12.8	36.08	21.61	-8.4	4.96	12.1	298.69	28.4
1958	583.65	436.89	583.65	34.0	27.95	20.00	38.6	3.43	20.9	310.97	28.9
1959	679.36	574.46	679.36	16.4	34.31	19.38	19.7	2.85	19.8	339.02	29.4

Year											
1960	685.47	566.05	615.89	- 9.3	32.21	20.46	- 6.3	3.32	19.1	369.87	29.8
1961	743.91	610.25	731.14	18.7	31.91	21.28	21.1	2.91	22.9	385.82	30.0
1962	726.01	535.76	652.10	-10.8	36.43	22.09	- 7.8	3.39	17.9	400.97	30.4
1963	767.21	646.79	762.95	17.0	41.21	23.20	20.6	3.04	18.5	425.90	30.9
1964	891.71	766.08	874.13	14.6	46.43	25.38	17.9	2.09	16.5	417.39	31.2
1965	969.26	840.59	969.26	10.9	53.67	28.61	14.1	2.95	18.1	453.27	31.8
1966	995.15	744.32	785.69	-18.9	57.68	31.89	-15.7	4.06	13.6	475.92	32.9
1967	943.08	786.41	905.11	15.2	53.87	30.19	19.0	3.34	16.8	476.50	33.9
1968	985.21	825.13	943.75	4.3	57.89	31.34	7.7	3.32	16.3	521.08	35.5
1969	968.85	769.93	800.35	-15.2	57.02	33.90	-11.6	4.24	14.0	542.25	37.7
1970	842.00	631.16	838.92	4.8	51.02	31.53	8.8	3.76	16.4	573.15	39.7
1971	950.82	797.97	890.20	6.1	55.09	30.86	9.8	3.47	16.2	607.61	41.1
1972	1,036.27	889.15	1,020.02	14.6	67.11	32.27	18.2	3.16	15.2	642.87	42.5
1973	1,051.70	788.31	850.86	16.6	86.17	35.33	-13.1	4.15	9.9	690.23	46.2
1974	891.66	577.60	616.24	-27.6	99.04	37.72	-23.1	6.12	6.2	746.95	51.9
1975	881.81	632.00	852.41	38.3	75.66	37.46	44.4	4.39	11.3	783.61	55.5
1976	1,014.79	858.70	1,004.65	17.9	96.72	41.40	22.7	4.12	10.4	798.20	58.2
1977	999.80	800.85	831.17	-17.3	89.10	45.84	-12.7	5.52	9.3	841.76	62.1
1978	906.44	742.72	805.01	- 3.1	112.79	48.52	2.7	6.03	7.1	890.69	67.7
1979	897.61	796.67	838.74	4.2	124.46	50.98	10.5	6.08	6.7	859.41	76.7
1980	1,000.20	759.98	963.99	14.9	121.86	54.36	21.3	5.64	7.9	928.50	86.2
1981	1,024.05	824.01	875.00	- 9.2	113.71	56.22	- 3.4	6.43	7.7	975.59	93.9
1982	1,070.55	776.92	1,046.54	19.6	9.15	54.14	25.8	5.17	*	881.51	97.6
1983	1,287.20	1,027.00	1,258.64	20.3	72.45	56.33	25.7	4.48	17.4	888.21	101.3
1984	1,286.60	1,086.60	1,211.57	- 3.7	113.58	60.63	1.1	5.00	10.7	916.70	105.3
1985	1,553.10	1,176.79	1,546.67	27.7	96.11	62.03	32.8	4.01	16.1	944.97	109.3
1986	1,955.57	1,502.29	1,895.95	22.6	115.59	67.04	26.9	3.54	16.4	986.48	110.5
1987	2,722.42	1,738.74	1,938.83	2.3	133.05	71.20	6.0	3.67	14.6	1,008.95	115.4
1988	2,183.50	1,879.14	2,168.57	11.8	215.46	79.53	16.0	3.67	10.1	1,075.47	120.6
1989	2,791.41	2,144.64	2,753.20	27.0	221.48	103.00	31.7	3.74	12.4	1,276.14	126.1
1990	2,999.75	2,365.10	2,633.66	- 4.3	172.05	103.70	- 0.6	3.94	15.3	1,340.00E	133.8
Increase 1926-1990:											
	+1,700%	+1,649%	+1,581%	—	+1,411%	+1,772%	—	—	—	+1,682%	+647%

E = Estimated   *Not meaningful

Note: Book values are based on net tangible assets per share. All data are adjusted to a basis consistent with the average.

Source: Johnson's Charts

Table 8.3
Standard & Poor's 500 Stock Index 65-Year Performance (1926–1990)

Year	High	Low	Close	Annual Change	Dividend	Year-End Yield	Annual Total Return	5-Year Average Rate of Return	Earnings	Year-End P-E Ratio	Consumer Price Index 1982–84 = 100	CPI % Annual Change
1925	—	—	12.71	—	—	—	—	—	—	—	17.9	—
1926	13.66	10.93	13.49	6.1%	.69	5.08%	11.6%	—	1.24	10.88	17.7	– 1.5
1927	17.71	13.18	17.71	31.3	.77	4.34	37.0	—	1.11	15.91	17.3	– 2.1
1928	24.35	16.95	24.35	37.5	.85	3.51	42.3	—	1.38	17.64	17.1	– 1.0
1929	31.92	17.66	21.45	–11.9	.97	4.53	–7.9	—	1.61	13.32	17.2	0.1
1930	25.92	14.44	14.34	–28.5	.98	6.37	–24.4	—	.97	15.81	16.1	– 6.0
1931	18.17	7.72	8.12	–47.1	.82	10.07	–41.7	– 3.9%	.61	13.31	14.6	– 9.5
1932	9.31	4.40	6.89	–15.1	.50	7.26	– 9.0	– 8.1	.41	16.60	13.1	–10.3
1933	12.20	5.53	10.10	46.6	.44	4.38	53.0	– 7.5	.44	22.95	13.1	0.5
1934	11.82	8.36	9.50	– 5.9	.45	4.75	–1.5	– 6.9	.49	19.39	13.4	2.0
1935	13.46	8.06	13.43	41.4	.47	3.53	46.3	3.2	.76	17.67	13.8	3.0
1936	17.69	13.40	17.18	27.9	.72	4.19	33.3	21.7	1.02	16.84	14.0	1.2
1937	18.68	10.17	10.55	–38.6	.80	7.62	–33.9	14.2	1.13	9.34	14.4	3.1
1938	13.79	8.50	13.21	25.2	.51	3.87	30.0	10.5	.64	20.64	14.0	– 2.8
1939	13.23	10.18	12.49	– 5.5	.62	4.94	– 0.8	10.7	.90	13.88	13.9	– 0.5
1940	12.77	8.99	10.58	–15.3	.67	6.34	– 9.9	0.5	1.05	10.08	14.1	1.0
1941	10.86	8.37	8.69	–17.9	.71	8.19	–11.2	– 5.7	1.16	7.49	15.5	9.7
1942	9.77	7.47	9.77	12.4	.59	5.99	19.2	4.2	1.03	9.49	16.9	9.3
1943	12.64	9.84	11.67	19.4	.61	5.25	25.7	3.5	.94	12.41	17.4	3.2
1944	13.29	11.56	13.28	13.8	.64	4.83	19.3	7.4	.93	14.28	17.8	2.1
1945	17.68	13.21	17.36	30.7	.66	3.81	43.2	17.8	.96	18.08	18.2	2.3
1946	19.25	14.12	15.30	–11.9	.71	4.61	– 7.8	18.7	1.06	14.43	21.5	18.2
1947	16.20	13.71	15.30	0.0	.84	5.52	5.5	15.9	1.61	9.50	23.4	9.0
1948	17.06	13.84	15.20	– 0.1	.93	6.14	5.4	11.9	2.29	6.64	24.1	2.7
1949	16.79	13.55	16.76	10.3	1.14	6.79	17.8	11.6	2.32	7.22	23.6	– 1.8
1950	20.43	16.65	20.41	21.8	1.47	7.20	30.5	9.5	2.84	7.19	25.0	5.8
1951	23.85	20.69	23.77	16.5	1.41	5.93	23.4	16.1	2.44	9.74	26.5	5.9
1952	26.59	23.09	26.57	11.8	1.41	5.29	17.7	18.7	2.40	11.07	26.7	0.9
1953	26.66	22.71	24.81	– 6.6	1.45	5.84	– 1.2	17.1	2.51	9.88	26.9	0.6
1954	35.98	24.80	35.98	45.0	1.54	4.28	51.2	23.1	2.77	12.99	26.7	– 0.5
1955	46.41	34.58	45.48	26.4	1.64	3.61	31.0	23.2	3.62	12.56	26.8	0.4
1956	49.74	43.11	46.67	2.6	1.74	3.73	6.4	19.6	3.41	13.69	27.6	2.9
1957	49.13	38.98	39.99	–14.3	1.79	4.48	–10.5	13.3	3.37	11.87	28.4	3.0
1958	55.21	40.33	55.21	38.1	1.75	3.17	42.4	21.8	2.89	19.10	28.9	1.8
1959	60.71	53.58	59.89	8.5	1.83	3.06	11.8	14.7	3.39	17.67	29.4	1.5

Year												
1960	60.39	52.30	55.85	− 6.7	1.95	3.35	−3.5	7.9	3.27	17.77	29.8	1.5
1961	72.64	57.57	71.55	28.1	2.02	2.82	31.7	12.6	3.19	22.43	30.0	0.7
1962	71.13	52.32	63.10	−11.8	2.13	3.38	−8.8	13.3	3.67	17.19	30.4	1.2
1963	75.02	62.69	75.02	18.9	2.28	3.04	22.5	9.9	4.02	18.66	30.9	1.6
1964	86.28	75.43	84.75	13.0	2.50	2.95	16.3	10.8	4.55	18.63	31.2	1.2
1965	92.63	81.60	92.43	9.1	2.72	2.94	12.3	14.2	5.19	17.81	31.8	1.9
1966	94.06	73.20	80.33	−13.1	2.87	3.57	−10.0	5.6	5.55	14.47	32.9	3.4
1967	97.59	80.38	96.47	20.1	2.92	3.03	23.7	12.2	5.33	18.10	33.9	3.0
1968	108.37	87.72	103.86	7.7	3.07	2.96	10.8	10.0	5.76	18.03	35.5	4.7
1969	106.16	89.20	92.06	−11.4	3.16	3.43	−8.3	4.9	5.78	15.93	37.7	6.1
1970	93.46	69.29	92.15	0.1	3.14	3.41	3.5	3.2	5.13	17.96	39.7	5.5
1971	104.77	90.16	102.09	10.8	3.07	3.01	14.1	8.2	5.70	17.91	41.1	3.4
1972	119.12	101.67	118.05	15.6	3.15	2.67	18.7	7.3	6.42	18.39	42.5	3.4
1973	120.24	92.16	97.55	−17.4	3.38	3.46	−14.5	1.9	8.16	11.95	46.2	8.8
1974	99.80	62.28	68.56	−29.7	3.60	5.25	−26.0	− 2.2	8.89	7.71	51.9	12.2
1975	95.61	70.04	90.19	31.5	3.68	4.08	36.9	3.2	7.96	11.33	55.5	7.0
1976	107.83	90.90	107.46	19.1	4.05	3.77	23.6	4.9	9.91	10.84	58.2	4.8
1977	107.00	90.71	95.10	−11.5	4.67	4.91	− 7.2	− 0.1	10.89	8.70	62.1	6.8
1978	106.99	86.90	96.11	1.1	5.07	5.28	6.4	4.3	12.33	7.79	67.7	9.0
1979	111.27	96.13	107.94	12.3	5.65	5.23	18.2	14.6	14.86	7.25	76.7	13.3
1980	140.52	98.22	135.76	25.8	6.16	4.54	31.5	13.8	14.82	9.19	86.2	12.4
1981	138.12	112.77	122.55	− 9.7	6.63	5.41	− 4.9	7.9	15.36	8.12	93.9	8.9
1982	143.02	102.42	140.64	14.8	6.87	4.88	20.4	13.6	12.64	11.12	97.6	3.9
1983	172.65	138.34	164.93	17.3	7.09	4.30	22.3	16.8	14.03	11.76	101.3	3.8
1984	169.28	147.82	167.24	1.4	7.53	4.50	6.0	14.3	16.64	10.05	105.3	4.0
1985	212.02	163.68	211.28	26.3	7.90	3.74	31.1	14.2	14.61	14.46	109.3	3.8
1986	254.00	203.49	242.17	14.6	8.28	3.42	18.5	19.4	14.43	16.72	110.5	1.1
1987	336.77	223.92	247.08	2.0	8.81	3.57	5.7	16.3	17.50	14.12	115.4	4.4
1988	283.66	242.63	277.72	12.4	9.73	3.50	16.3	15.1	23.76	11.69	120.6	4.4
1989	359.80	275.31	353.40	27.3	11.05	3.13	31.2	20.2	22.90	15.43	126.1	4.6
1990	368.95	295.46	330.22	− 6.6	12.10	3.66	− 3.1	13.1	21.60E	15.29	133.8	6.1

Increase 1926–1990:

	+2,601%	+2,603%	+2,498%	—	+1,654%	—	—	—	+1,642%	—	+647%	—

E = Estimated

Compounded Annual Rates of Return

5 Years	1986–1990	13.1	20 Years	1971–1990	10.9	40 Years	1951–1990	11.5
10 Years	1981–1990	13.7	25 Years	1966–1990	9.1	50 Years	1941–1990	11.8
15 Years	1976–1990	13.7	30 Years	1961–1990	10.2	65 Years	1926–1990	10.0

Table 8.4
The Changing Dow

Stocks Dropped Since 1964	Stocks Added Since 1964
Chrysler	Philip Morris
Esmark	McDonald's
American Brands	Coca-Cola
Johns-Manville	Merck
Owens-Illinois	American Express
International Nickel	Boeing
Anaconda	Minnesota Mining & Manufacturing
General Foods	IBM
Navistar	Caterpillar
Primerica	Disney
USX	J.P. Morgan

increased only about 50%. Obviously, if stock prices increased almost two and one-half times, while dividends were almost doubling and earnings were increasing only 50%, the stockholder was doing better than his company. The more worrisome fact, therefore, is in the P-E ratio column, which shows that from the end of 1979 to the end of 1989, the P-E ratio of the S&P 500 more than doubles from 7.25 to 15.43 times the earnings. Remember, the P-E ratio is the most commonly used analytical tool in stock selection.

This background should dampen optimistic forecasts for stock prices in the 1990s. Certainly, it would be nice if the consumer price index continued to decline, but we are going into the 1990s at a rate of 4.6% instead of 12%. If you look over historic year-end P-E ratios on table 8.3, it is pretty hard to conclude that it will double again and reach 30 times earnings at the end of the 1990s. It, therefore, appears that more of the gains in the 1990s from common stocks are going to have to come from earnings and dividends rather than increasing P-E ratios and reduced inflation.

I have inferred that common stock investment is likely to exaggerate changes in the cost of living over a period of time. Now, we might move from history and spend a moment on the logic of this occurrence by remembering that the purchase of common stock is actually nothing more than the purchase of a proportionate share of ownership in a company. Therefore, we own our share of the physical assets of the company, its inventories, its plant and equipment—everything that the company owns—and a share of its liabilities. The values reflected on the balance sheet of the company are historical and, in an inflationary world, adjusting the book value of our stock to current values can be a satisfying exercise. Most companies—but not all—are able to produce somewhat higher earnings as a product of inflation than they otherwise would. For one thing, we stockholders may well be the beneficiaries of inventory profits. Second, most companies have at least some element of fixed costs in their P&L statements, which work to their benefit during a period when they can raise the selling prices of their products. Third, most of our companies have leverage in the form of debt in their balance sheets, which has a tendency to work for the company in an inflationary world. Spend a moment thinking about a particular company and what happens to it in an inflationary environment. Rapidly changing rates of inflation, however, can present real problems for business. As a businessman, my hope for inflation in the 1990s is that the rate will remain at least stable, whatever the rate is.

Back to the contest. I will give you my entry: I guess that common stocks will not perform as well in the 1990s as they did in the 1980s, but I also guess that they will appreciate more than the rate of inflation. I will spare you the qualitative reasoning and simply guess that 60% in common stocks and 40% in lendings are a reasonable approach for the entry form.

Having filed my entry, I will leave the game for a decade, but it would not displease me if you now have the impression that protecting your purchasing power over a period of time can be a tough challenge and requires the use of a fair degree of ownership. At times, this game is very, very hard. The DJIA closed 1964 at 874.13 and 1981 at 875.00, a gain of less than a point in 17 years! Not a bad case for studying Chinese ceramics.

If our sponsor had been a saver instead of a spender and let us reinvest income, the game would have been substantially easier. If you save all your income, you may be able to be conservative and still keep up with inflation. Of course, the assumptions are that you do not spend any of your income and you do not even pay taxes on it. Those are not easy assumptions, but you can see how the saver has an enormous advantage.

I designed these exercises not with the idea of convincing you to become a more conservative or a more aggressive investor but with the idea of providing you with a better context in which to evaluate what kind of investor you are and possibly what kind of investor you would like to be. It is statistically unlikely that the 1990s will turn out as either you or I forecast, but my hope is that you now have a better framework for "the world in which we live."

It is useful to create a mental framework for inflation and the challenges of investing your assets. The concepts and interrelationships between inflation, lending, and ownership are important enough to reiterate some of the conclusions we have considered for your framework. We invest for the future and generally to protect or augment the purchasing power of our assets. As a result, the rate of inflation has a substantial impact on our investments over a period of time. During the 1980s, the rate of inflation declined enormously in this country, but the threat of worsening inflation is as strong as the prospect for further improvement. Against this background, we have the inability of the lending approach, our bond buying, to fight inflation unless we are dedicated savers and forgo the pleasures of using the income from our lendings. This leads to the unfortunate necessity of taking risks to increase our assets and in turn to maintain our purchasing power. Thus, we look to ownership as our approach to fight inflation. The first question we must consider is what type of ownership. Certain unusual material goods investments have done very well, but some of the more common approaches have been disappointing. Selecting a material goods or real estate niche can, therefore, be a speculative approach. Common stocks are probably as forecastable a means of addressing the ownership question as we can find. Both the historical and qualitative cases for common stocks indicate that they have been, and should continue to be, good investments in an inflationary world. Nevertheless, there have been protracted periods in which stocks have done poorly, and we enter the 1990s after a decade of rather outstanding results. Therefore, as a note of caution, we might bear in mind that future results in common stock investing could well require consistently better records of corporate earnings and dividends.

•

Flunking Myself...

If I were a college student wanting to embarrass the author, I would focus on this chapter and start my attack by expressing the belief that, contrary to the opening comment (this chapter is important), there in fact was nothing important at all. As the author, I am embarrassed by my forecasts, and while writing the critique, I was tempted to place the critique before the original and pretend the original was never written. In a nutshell, I spent a great deal of chapter 8 being wrong.

The concepts we addressed, however, were not entirely useless; therefore, let's review history for a moment and then see how the world has changed and how we might amend chapter 8.

Ten years ago a major portion of American investors still lived and invested in the shadow of the Depression. Despite the ascension of common stocks in the 1980s, far greater numbers of Americans were lending their money rather than acquiring ownership. The high inflation rates of the 1970s had certainly given stockbrokers like myself ammunition to convert a nation of lenders at least partially into a nation of stockholders. The reasoning behind this shift centered on inflation and the growing conviction of investors that fixed income investing, comfortable as it was, would not protect the purchasing power of our assets if we expected to hang around for a while. Certainly the high inflation years of the seventies frightened fixed income investors and promoted the concept of using owner-ship to fight inflation.

The original aim of chapter 8 was to do an exercise, to give you kids a rational approach toward allocating your assets, fixed income versus common stocks, that could be considered conservative while allowing you to maintain your purchasing power over time.

The conclusion of the 50/50 breakdown between stocks and bonds was based on a history of comparative returns, the history of inflation, and a bit of common sense. From this 50/50 base, the investor could easily adjust to becoming more aggressive (trying to make more money) or more conservative (less dedicated to fight-ing inflation).

We have updated tables 8.2 and 8.3, which merit more than a glance even today. Note particularly in tables 8.2-2 and 8.3-2 the annual changes in stock prices during the late 1980s and the 1990s versus the consumer price index annual change. It was primarily from history that I made my forecast of 6% for inflation and perhaps 10% on stock prices for the 1990s. Let me repeat a 1989 paragraph to show what a terrible forecaster I was:

> This background should dampen optimistic forecasts for stock prices in the 1990s. Certainly, it would be nice if the consumer price index continued to decline, but we are going into the 1990s at a rate of 4.6% instead of 12%. If you look over historic year-end P-E ratios on table 8.3, it is pretty hard to conclude that they will double again and reach 30 times earnings at the end of the 1990s. It therefore appears that more of the gains in the 1990s from common stocks are going to have to come from earnings and dividends rather than increasing P-E ratios and reduced inflation.

Everything I regarded as unlikely is exactly what happened. The inflation rate declined substantially, and the price-earnings ratios shown in table 8.3 doubled again and reached 30 times earn-ings before the end of the 1990s. Finally, the increases in common stock prices despite the good earnings in the nineties were perhaps

75% a product of stock price increases and only 25% a product of increased earnings.

Today our inflation rate is so low that investors generally don't spend any time thinking about it. We probably could have hedged inflation in the 1990s with 15% of our assets in stocks. Fortunately for my clients, I erred on the stock side instead of the bond side. The most we can say is that a few of us worry about the resurgence of inflation and its negative impact on the stock market.

I mentioned in the original that the stockholder fared better in the 1980s than his company. His stock price increased much more than his earnings and dividends. Therefore the price-earnings ratio doubled. The same thing happened in the 1990s. Wonderful but scary!

What do we learn from being so inept? Certainly it reiterates my contention that we should not try to forecast the stock market. Certainly also in the setting of investment policy, the impact of the inflation factor is far less today than it has been in the past. If nothing else, a little time with exhibits that trace the market, its annual changes, year-end P-E ratios, and the changes in the cost of living proves very thought-provoking. I made the comment earlier that we Americans always expect that what's going on at the moment will continue forever. It won't.

Table 8.2-2
Dow Jones Industrial Average 53-Year Performance (1947–1999)

Year	Market			Annual Change	Earnings	Dividends	Annual Total Return	Year-End Yield	Year-End P-E Multiple	Consumer Price Index 1982–84 = 100
	High	Low	Close							
1946	—	—	177.20	—	13.63	7.50	—	—	—	21.5
1947	186.85	163.21	181.16	2.2	18.80	9.21	7.4	5.08	9.6	23.4
1948	193.16	165.39	177.30	-2.1	23.07	11.50	4.2	6.49	7.7	24.1
1949	200.52	161.60	200.13	12.9	23.54	12.79	20.1	6.39	8.5	23.6
1950	235.47	196.81	235.41	17.6	30.70	16.13	25.7	6.85	7.7	25.0
1951	276.37	238.99	269.23	14.4	26.59	16.34	21.3	6.07	10.1	26.5
1952	292.00	256.35	291.90	8.4	24.78	15.48	14.2	5.30	11.8	26.7
1953	293.79	255.49	289.90	-3.8	27.23	16.11	4.8	5.56	10.7	26.9
1954	404.39	279.87	404.39	39.5	28.18	17.47	45.5	4.32	14.4	26.7
1955	488.40	388.20	488.40	20.8	35.78	21.58	26.1	4.41	13.7	26.8
1956	521.05	462.35	499.47	2.3	33.34	22.99	7.0	4.60	15.0	27.6
1957	520.77	419.79	435.69	-12.8	36.08	21.61	- 8.4	4.96	12.1	28.4
1958	583.65	436.89	583.65	34.0	27.95	20.00	38.6	3.43	20.9	28.9
1959	679.36	574.46	679.36	16.4	34.31	19.38	19.7	2.85	19.8	29.4
1960	685.47	566.05	615.89	- 9.3	32.21	20.46	- 6.3	3.32	19.1	29.8
1961	734.91	610.25	731.14	18.7	31.91	21.28	21.1	2.91	22.9	30.0
1962	726.01	535.76	652.10	-10.8	36.43	22.09	- 7.8	3.39	17.9	30.4
1963	767.21	646.79	762.95	17.0	41.21	23.20	20.6	3.04	18.5	30.9
1964	891.71	766.08	874.13	14.6	46.43	25.38	17.9	2.09	16.5	31.2
1965	969.26	840.59	969.26	10.9	53.67	28.61	14.1	2.95	18.1	31.8
1966	995.15	744.32	785.69	-18.9	57.68	31.89	-15.7	4.06	13.6	32.9
1967	943.08	786.41	905.11	15.2	53.87	30.19	19.0	3.34	16.8	33.9
1968	985.21	825.13	943.75	4.3	57.89	31.34	7.7	3.32	16.3	35.5
1969	968.85	769.93	800.35	-15.2	57.02	33.90	-11.6	4.24	14.0	37.7
1970	842.00	631.16	838.92	4.8	51.02	31.53	8.8	3.76	16.4	39.7
1971	950.82	797.97	890.20	6.1	55.09	30.86	9.8	3.47	16.2	41.1
1972	1,036.27	889.15	1,020.02	14.6	67.11	32.27	18.2	3.16	15.2	42.5
1973	1,051.70	788.31	850.86	-16.6	86.17	35.33	-13.1	4.15	9.9	46.2
1974	891.66	577.60	616.24	-27.6	99.04	37.72	-23.1	6.12	6.2	51.9

Year									
1975	881.81	632.00	852.41	38.3	75.66	37.46	44.4	4.39	11.3	55.5
1976	1,014.79	858.70	1,004.65	17.9	96.72	41.40	22.7	4.12	10.4	58.2
1977	999.80	800.85	831.17	-17.3	89.10	45.84	-12.7	5.52	9.3	62.1
1978	906.44	742.72	805.01	- 3.1	112.79	48.52	2.7	6.03	7.1	67.7
1979	897.61	796.67	838.74	4.2	124.46	50.98	10.5	6.08	6.7	76.7
1980	1,000.20	759.98	963.99	14.9	121.86	54.36	21.3	5.64	7.9	86.2
1981	1,024.05	824.01	875.00	- 9.2	113.71	56.22	- 3.4	6.43	7.7	93.9
1982	1,070.55	776.92	1,046.54	19.6	9.15	54.14	25.8	5.17	*	97.6
1983	1,287.20	1,027.00	1,258.64	20.3	72.45	56.33	25.7	4.48	17.4	101.3
1984	1,286.60	1,086.60	1,211.57	- 3.7	113.58	60.63	1.1	5.00	10.7	105.3
1985	1,553.10	1,176.79	1,546.67	27.7	96.11	62.03	32.8	4.01	16.1	109.3
1986	1,955.57	1,502.29	1,895.95	22.6	115.59	67.04	26.9	3.54	16.4	110.5
1987	2,722.42	1,738.74	1,938.83	2.3	133.05	71.20	6.0	3.67	14.6	115.4
1988	2,183.50	1,879.14	2,168.57	11.8	215.46	79.53	16.0	3.67	10.1	120.6
1989	2,791.41	2,144.64	2,753.20	27.0	221.48	103.00	31.7	3.74	12.4	126.1
1990	2,999.75	2,365.10	2,633.66	- 4.3	172.05	103.70	- 0.6	3.94	15.3	133.8
1991	3,168.83	2,470.30	3,168.83	20.3	49.27	95.18	23.9	3.00	64.3	137.9
1992	3,413.21	3,136.58	3,301.11	4.2	108.25	100.72	7.4	3.05	30.5	141.9
1993	3,794.33	3,241.95	3,754.09	13.7	146.82	99.66	16.7	2.65	25.6	145.8
1994	3,978.36	3,593.35	3,834.44	2.1	256.13	105.66	5.0	2.76	15.0	149.7
1995	5,216.47	3,832.08	5,117.12	33.5	311.02	116.56	36.5	2.28	16.5	153.5
1996	6,560.91	5,032.94	6,448.27	26.0	353.88	131.14	28.6	2.03	18.2	158.6
1997	8,259.31	6,391.69	7,908.25	22.6	391.29	136.10	24.8	1.72	20.2	161.3
1998	9,374.26	7,539.07	9,181.43	16.1	383.35	151.13	18.0	1.65	24.0	163.9
1999	11,497.12	9,120.67	11,497.12	25.22	477.22	168.52	27.1	1.47	24.1	168.8
Increase 1947–99:			+6,388%		+3,401%	+2,147%				+683%

*Not meaningful

Note: Book values are based on net tangible assets per share. All data are adjusted to a basis consistent with the average.

Table 8.3-2
Standard & Poor's 500 Stock Index 53-Year Performance (1947–1999)

Year	High	Low	Close	Annual Change	Dividend	Year-End Yield	Annual Total Return	5-Year Average Rate of Return	Earnings	Year-End P-E Ratio	Consumer Price Index 1982–84 = 100	CPI % Annual Change
1946	—	—	15.30	—	.71	—	—	—	1.06	—	21.5	—
1947	16.20	13.71	15.30	0.0	.84	5.52	5.5	15.9	1.61	9.50	23.4	9.0
1948	17.06	13.84	15.20	- 0.7	.93	6.14	5.4	11.9	2.29	6.64	24.1	2.7
1949	16.79	13.55	16.76	10.3	1.14	6.79	17.8	11.6	2.32	7.22	23.6	- 1.8
1950	20.43	16.65	20.41	21.8	1.47	7.20	30.5	9.5	2.84	7.19	25.0	5.8
1951	23.85	20.69	23.77	16.5	1.41	5.93	23.4	16.1	2.44	9.74	26.5	5.9
1952	26.59	23.09	26.57	11.8	1.41	5.29	17.7	18.7	2.40	11.07	26.7	0.9
1953	26.66	22.71	24.81	- 6.6	1.45	5.84	- 1.2	17.1	2.51	9.88	26.9	0.6
1954	35.98	24.80	35.98	45.0	1.54	4.28	51.2	23.1	2.77	12.99	26.7	- 0.5
1955	46.41	34.58	45.48	26.4	1.64	3.61	31.0	23.2	3.62	12.56	26.8	0.4
1956	49.74	43.11	46.67	2.6	1.74	3.73	6.4	19.6	3.41	13.69	27.6	2.9
1957	49.13	38.98	39.99	-14.3	1.79	4.48	-10.5	13.3	3.37	11.87	28.4	3.0
1958	55.21	40.33	55.21	38.1	1.75	3.17	42.4	21.8	2.89	19.10	28.9	1.8
1959	60.71	53.58	59.89	8.5	1.83	3.06	11.8	14.7	3.39	17.67	29.4	1.5
1960	60.39	52.30	55.85	- 3.0	1.95	3.35	- 0.3	7.9	3.27	17.77	29.8	1.5
1961	72.64	57.57	71.55	23.1	2.02	2.82	26.6	12.6	3.19	22.43	30.0	0.7
1962	71.13	52.32	63.10	-11.8	2.13	3.38	- 8.8	13.3	3.67	17.19	30.4	1.2
1963	75.02	62.69	75.02	18.9	2.28	3.04	22.5	9.9	4.02	18.66	30.9	1.6
1964	86.28	75.43	84.75	13.0	2.50	2.95	16.3	10.8	4.55	18.63	31.2	1.2
1965	92.63	81.60	92.43	9.1	2.72	2.94	12.3	14.2	5.19	17.81	31.8	1.9
1966	94.06	73.20	80.33	-13.1	2.87	3.57	-10.0	5.6	5.55	14.47	32.9	3.4
1967	97.59	80.38	96.47	20.1	2.92	3.03	23.7	12.2	5.33	18.10	33.9	3.0
1968	108.37	87.72	103.86	7.7	3.07	2.96	10.8	10.0	5.76	18.03	35.5	4.7
1969	106.16	89.20	92.06	-11.4	3.16	3.43	- 8.3	4.9	5.78	15.93	37.7	6.1
1970	93.46	69.29	92.15	0.1	3.14	3.41	3.5	3.2	5.13	17.96	39.7	5.5
1971	104.77	90.16	102.09	10.8	3.07	3.01	14.1	8.2	5.70	17.91	41.1	3.4
1972	119.12	101.67	118.05	15.6	3.15	2.67	18.7	7.3	6.42	18.39	42.5	3.4
1973	120.24	92.16	97.55	-17.4	3.38	3.46	-14.5	1.9	8.16	11.95	46.2	8.8
1974	99.80	62.28	68.56	-29.7	3.60	5.25	-26.0	- 2.2	8.89	7.71	51.9	12.2

Year												
1975	95.61	70.04	90.19	31.5	3.68	4.08	36.9	3.2	7.96	11.33	55.5	7.0
1976	107.83	90.90	107.46	19.1	4.05	3.77	23.6	4.9	9.91	10.84	58.2	4.8
1977	107.00	90.71	95.10	-11.5	4.67	4.91	- 7.2	- 0.1	10.89	8.70	62.1	6.8
1978	106.99	86.90	96.11	1.1	5.07	5.28	6.4	4.3	12.33	7.79	67.7	9.0
1979	111.27	96.13	107.94	12.3	5.65	5.23	18.2	14.6	14.86	7.25	76.7	13.3
1980	140.52	98.22	135.76	25.8	6.16	4.54	31.5	13.8	14.82	9.19	86.2	12.4
1981	138.12	112.77	122.55	- 9.7	6.63	5.41	- 4.9	7.9	15.36	8.12	93.9	8.9
1982	143.02	102.42	140.64	14.8	6.87	4.88	20.4	13.6	12.64	11.12	97.6	3.9
1983	172.65	138.34	164.93	17.3	7.09	4.30	22.3	16.8	14.03	11.76	101.3	3.8
1984	169.28	147.82	167.24	1.4	7.53	4.50	6.0	14.3	16.64	10.05	105.3	4.0
1985	212.02	163.68	211.28	26.3	7.90	3.74	31.1	14.2	14.61	14.46	109.3	3.8
1986	254.00	203.49	242.17	14.6	8.28	3.42	18.5	19.4	14.43	16.72	110.5	1.1
1987	336.77	223.92	247.08	2.0	8.81	3.57	5.7	16.3	17.50	14.12	115.4	4.4
1988	283.66	242.63	277.72	12.4	9.73	3.50	16.3	15.1	23.76	11.69	126.1	4.4
1989	359.80	275.31	353.40	27.3	11.05	3.13	31.2	20.2	22.87	15.43	126.1	4.6
1990	368.95	295.46	330.22	- 6.6	12.10	3.66	- 3.1	13.1	21.34	15.29	133.8	6.1
1991	417.09	311.49	417.09	26.3	12.20	2.93	30.0	15.2	15.97	25.89	137.9	3.1
1992	441.28	394.50	435.71	4.5	12.38	2.84	7.4	15.6	19.09	22.82	141.9	2.9
1993	470.94	429.05	466.45	7.1	12.58	2.70	9.9	14.3	21.88	21.32	145.8	2.7
1994	482.00	438.92	459.27	- 1.5	13.18	2.87	1.3	8.6	30.60	15.01	149.7	2.7
1995	621.69	459.11	615.93	34.1	13.79	2.24	37.1	16.3	34.09	18.02	153.5	2.5
1996	757.03	598.48	740.74	20.3	14.90	2.01	22.7	15.0	39.29	18.85	158.6	3.3
1997	983.79	737.01	970.43	31.0	15.49	1.60	33.1	20.0	40.23	24.1	161.3	1.7
1998	1244.93	912.83	1229.23	26.7	16.20	1.32	28.3	24.5	37.71	32.27	163.9	1.6
1999	1506.91	1136.89	1469.25	19.5	16.69	1.14	20.9	28.4	48.17	33.42	168.3	2.7
Increase 1947–1999:			+9,503%		+2,251%				+4,444%		+683%	

99

CHAPTER 9

You, Wonderful You

YOU ARE UNIQUE AND YOUR INVESTMENT POLICY SHOULD BE uniquely suited to you. From your balance sheet, you know your financial situation quantitatively, you have some awareness of your saving/spending patterns, and you now have some feel for what you can expect from different investments. Each of us has distinct financial needs that we should consider as we build our investment policy, so let's think about you *qualitatively* for a few minutes.

Portfolio managers who do not know you personally are handicapped in helping to solve your financial problems. We have all read articles that suggest in general terms a certain investment approach of the moment, for example, we should be 20% in cash, 40% in bonds, and 40% in stocks. Maybe the writer should be 40% in stocks and bonds and 20% in cash, or maybe his kids should be, but how does he know what either you or I should be? I want to be where I should be for me, and I want you to be where you should be for you. For example, at one time I was a private in the army with a wife and two kids, making $132 a month. Years before, my grandfather had been kind enough to set up a small trust for me, which the bank trustee invested 100% in tax-free bonds. Certainly, income was a serious subject for me and my young family, but, in our zero-tax-bracket situation, there was no need for it to be tax free. Obviously, the bank trustee had never met me.

Probably no one can identify all the qualitative factors that relate to you and your investment policy as well as you can, but I can mention a few of the obvious factors and let you think about your own situation. Of course, you may be more than just you. You may be part of a whole family and two or three generations may be involved in your thinking. If you are part of a family, talking about these subjects for a few minutes at the dinner table is not a bad approach. Mid-January is a good time for this, since most of us do not have much to talk about at the dinner table then. Only two cities in the nation will be represented at the Super Bowl, so all the rest of us can talk about something else. Furthermore, in mid-January you should have finished your year-end balance sheet, and there is plenty of time left in the year to do something about it.

Let's get the unpleasant subjects out of the way first and make a list of those—it is hoped, few—events that could have very serious financial implications for the family. *Who produces the income for this sumptuous meal, and what happens to the rest of the group if something happens to those who provide this income? What if they die or become incapacitated? What other terrible event could occur with enormous financial implications? What if one of us hits somebody with a car or somebody is very seriously injured coming up the front steps?* Well, we cannot buy insurance against all the terrible things that can happen in life, but we can buy insurance against most of the terrible financial things that can happen to us. My basic philosophy on insurance is to buy it for those events that can really have enormously adverse financial impacts on us, whether it is life insurance, health insurance, car insurance, or personal liability insurance. Forget about the little things like your dented right-front fender.

In today's world, your individual or family situation can vary greatly. I understand we now live in a world in which only 10% of American families have the male as the breadwinner taking care of the spouse, who does the housework and raises the children. What was once regarded as the typical American family is not typical any-more. What do we want to protect through insurance? Obviously, our assets and our income. Once we have anticipated terrible financial events, we can think about how to insure against them. The answers will vary, from the extreme of those who must dedicate all their savings to life insurance to the other extreme of those who, in the event their spouse dies, can return to wealthy parents. I would emphasize two points. First, your insurance program should be as unique and specific as your investment policy. Second, if all your annual savings must be dedicated to averting economic tragedies, then insurance is the place to spend them, and you can quit worrying about what stock to buy for a while.

Fortunately, you will find that some insurance, for example, personal liability, is still a minor budget item. You will also find that there are many different approaches to such a common need as life insurance. I am not as opposed to life insurance which builds permanent values as are most people in the securities industry. Stockbrokers frequently advocate buying the cheapest kind of life insurance and investing the difference. Frankly, many people I know who do buy cheap insurance blow the difference. I hope you will be so successful that what you spend on life insurance will become a minor budget item as time goes by, and you will probably be glad you bought some insurance with permanent values.

Next, you might have a lively discussion on the subject of *financial goals* and let each member of the group throw in his two cents' worth. You might divide these goals into *long term* and *short term*, since most of us may make some sizable expenditures in the near future. In the context of a lifetime, getting the kids through college may be one interim goal, albeit an important one. As a married PFC in the army, I could afford to do little more than have kids, which run about a dollar a pound in the army. The ultimate result was three kids, who barely qualified for America's most expensive colleges, all at roughly the same time. Needless to say, the situation led to a little pencil pushing in advance. There is no rule against using pencil and pad as you discuss some of these challenges, even at the dinner table.

Talking about long- and short-term goals can be fun, but then the question comes up as to how realistic these goals are and how we can actually attain them. Therefore, I will mention a few considerations common to all of us. You should consider each factor and how you believe it should affect *your* investment policy.

Your *age* and *health* can give you some idea of your *life expectancy*, which helps indicate how aggressively or conservatively you invest your assets. You might take another glance at table 2.1 (page 20) in case you cannot remember how long you are supposed to live. You might then relate your own life expectancy to *how long you expect to work and produce income*, assuming you do. Through this simple exercise, you will gain some feel for the practicality of your longer-term goals. For your discussion, I will also offer this thought: Younger people have a tendency to get too aggressive too soon, and older people have a tendency to get too conservative too soon. In my family, all of us who are over 39 consider ourselves to be only 39 and, therefore, at a good age to be aggressive. If retirement is a strong goal for you within a decade or so, I recommend that you use that pencil and pad to do a little calculation of your income at the point you retire and relate it to the inflation rate between now and then. (We'll do some calculating together in a moment.)

Another factor to which not enough people pay enough attention is the *nature of their occupation* and the *stability of their income*. Too many of my friends worked for large corporations, had good jobs, and found themselves unexpectedly out of work as a product of what happened within the corporation. As another illustration, I suggest that a healthy, tenured schoolteacher with a high certainty of stable income and a growing pension plan can have a considerably more aggressive investment policy than a commissioned salesman in a cyclical industry. Measure your own situation relative to the question of income stability as well as the amount of income needed.

The *size of your net worth* unquestionably should have an impact on your investment policy. If you do not have much, it gets a little serious when you lose some. If you have a bunch, it allows you more freedom to assume a higher level of risk. I will throw in a couple of observations. People who have always had a lot of money are sometimes too conservative in their investments because they are afraid of losing it and don't know what the world is like without it. People who have started from modest beginnings and built a fortune can frequently invest more aggressively because they know they were just as happy before they had a bunch. Another observation is that savers, if they know themselves well, can assume more risk and presumably reap more rewards simply because they know they will rebuild their assets if they lose some of them. In many cases, however, the savers tend to be overly conservative investors, maybe because they worked hard to be savers and do not want to lose it.

The next point to discuss might be the income you want to generate from your investments and when you want to generate it. Americans often do not distinguish between *want and need* in the *production of income*. Americans like income, whether they need it or not, and do not seem to grasp the trade-off, which is to give up appreciation. Sometimes I think Americans are happier if they are getting 7% income a year with no appreciation from their investments than they are if they get only 3 1/2% every year while their assets are doubling every five years. My suggestion on income is to figure out what you *really need* from your investments and, once you have that covered, forget income and concentrate on long-term goals, such as building your net worth. Of course, future income can be a very strong long-term goal. Retirement planning is a great subject on which to do some income calculations combined with your life expectancy and time left to build assets before you retire. Figure out how long you are likely to live and how long you are likely to work. Then, figure out what your social security and pension benefits will be and what income you will need from your investments. Then, go back to those inflation tables and make adjustments in all your figures for inflation between now and when you retire, and now and when you die. Unless you are really old and rich, this is a very worthy exercise and you are silly not to do it. I suspect for many of us these figures could provide a pretty good incentive to save.

Next, you might discuss *your tax situation* and how it should impact your investment policy. For most of us, what we can or should do to reduce or control tax payments is more of a short-term strategy than part of the basic policy. Nevertheless, there are mechanisms for deferring income and tax strategies that can be used successfully in our investing. Only Congress seems to ignore how tax policy influences our investing. We all hate to pay taxes, but sometimes we allow taxes to have too much rather than too little impact on our investment approach.

After dinner in front of the fire, you might discuss *your own psychological approach toward the assumption of risk versus reward*, your tolerance for pain versus your desire for gain. Your personal comfort with an investment such as an aggressive common stock should be a major factor in your policy and one that you should and can consider better than anyone else. Some people can handle every quantitative and qualitative factor, reach the logical conclusion that they should be quite aggressive in their investment policy, and then are simply unable to handle this psychologically. If a stock goes down a whole point in a day, it is really bothersome to some. Others can go through the crash of '87 with the reaction that it was sort of interesting. For example, not one but three of my little-old-lady clients called me within a couple of days after the October 1987 debacle. I asked them how they were and they said they were fine; each had called just to make sure I was fine. Good tough kids.

One of my theories relating to investment policy might be easier to understand for those of us who are older kids. After a certain point in life, maybe about halfway, a good many of us settle into a certain standard of living with which we are largely content. We do not change our lifestyle very much, and many of us really do not *want* to change our life-styles. This *pattern of living* has a certain annual cost to it, almost a fixed cost with an inflation adjustment and perhaps a small annual increment for a new extravagance like some new club we decide to join. If we have reached this point in life, we can use the awareness of the annual cost of this pattern to judge how we really want to model our investments for our future and perhaps that of our offspring.

Undoubtedly, you have factors in your personal financial situation that I have not raised that are important to you. My aim is not to tell you how you should think about these things but simply to make sure you do think about them. If more than one generation is involved, these discussions are likely to be more complex but perhaps more valuable. Table 9.1 contains a summary of the personal factors we have discussed so far in this book. You should review this list and consider whether each of these factors should lead you to be more aggressive or conservative than you are at the moment.

·

A New Century and You're Still Unique...

The original chapter 9 wasn't a bad chapter. Unlike most, it has not been obliterated by my lousy forecasts and the passage of time. What I was trying to do was get you thinking about yourself and possibly your children. You were to take the figures you put together on your balance sheet and your income versus expense calculations and perhaps use these to establish some reasonable goals for yourself or your family. Oddly enough, the personal factors I discussed still seem reasonable to me, including the comment "Younger people have a tendency to get too aggressive too soon, and older people have the tendency to get too conservative too soon."

A central question for you to consider is your own psychological approach to the assumption of risk. The fact that our bull market has been so wonderful for so long has left the younger kids untested psychologically by a miserable down market. This means we virtually have a generation of common stock owners who have to guess at their own reaction toward losing money as fast as or faster than they have made it.

Table 9.1

Summary of Personal Factors

I. Balance sheet / net worth factors
  A. Size of your net worth
  B. Classification of your major assets
  C. Your tax situation

II. Income factors
  A. Adequacy of your current income
  B. Nature of your occupation
  C. Stability and expectancy of your current income
  D. Wants vs. needs for investment income
  E. Your tax situation (again)

III. Insurance factors
  A. Insurance on income producer
    1. Life insurance
    2. Disability insurance
  B. Insurance on other terrible financial events
    1. Health insurance
    2. Liability insurance
    3. Auto insurance
    4. Property, casualty, and fire insurance

IV. Life habits and standard of living factors
  A. Your age
  B. Your health
  C. Your life expectancy
  D. Your risk tolerance
  E. Saver vs. spender
  F. Cost of your lifestyle

V. Additional factors

_____

_____

_____

_____

_____

_____

_____

The bull market has also had some substantial impacts on the older kids who have had at least a fair-size investment in common stocks for some years. Some have found themselves with increasing expenses and not a corresponding increase in their income. They visit me with the comment that their stocks are fine, but they need a bit more income. Explicitly they may need to spend 5% to 7% of their net worth annually to support their "pattern of living," and their portfolio is paying them only 2% or 3%. My advice has most frequently been to simply sell enough of their securities annually to raise the money needed instead of selling a bunch of their stocks, paying an equivalent bunch of taxes, and trying to buy higher-income-producing securities. This violates their promises to Mom and Dad not to spend principal, but it saves them from sending a barrel of money to Washington, D.C., to be wasted.

A wonderful businessman friend of mine considered the high levels of the market a couple of years ago and decided to sell all his publicly owned stocks. He knew the stock market was historically overpriced. Most people would now regard that as a terrible mistake, because the market has done so well over the last two years. Oddly enough, I think it was a reasonable decision. Based on his personal factors, he knew he had plenty of money to take care of all his wants and needs, his pattern of life was comfortably established, and his joy in making more money in the stock market had become minimal. A reasonable decision, but not a good one. What was his error? We'll criticize later.

Think about your wonderful self relative to the personal factors I mentioned (table 9.1), make some notes to yourself on other aspects of your world to be considered, and stay with me, kids.

CHAPTER 10

Setting Your Investment Policy

WE ARE GOING THROUGH THIS PROCESS SO THAT YOU WILL BE able to design and understand your investment plan. Parts of your plan could be described as short-term financial strategies. Examples of short-term strategies include buying a certain kind of insurance policy, withdrawing some of your money market fund to pay off your current debts, or paying for an impending college bill. Most of these decisions can be handled with a little thought and a few calculations to make intelligent trade-offs. Without getting too wrapped up in semantics, I will refer to your *investment policy* as that part of your plan that involves longer-term strategies and is generally more permanent in nature, i.e., how you invest your savings for your future major goals.

If there is a central aim from the establishment of your policy, it should be to allocate your assets among the investment alternatives we have discussed in such a way as to attain these longer-term, presumably practical goals you have established. Certainly, your policy will contain some strategies for each investment alternative, but *the focal point of an investment policy is asset allocation based primarily on the balance of risk to principal versus reward.*

The number of individuals who have come into my office over the last 30 years and told me they have seriously considered their own personal situation in the context of the external world and, therefore, can present me with a clear-cut investment policy is exactly zero. This is not a complaint on my part, because helping people establish their policies is frequently how I can help them best. Therefore, we can do it together. Establishing the policy is the part of this investment process in which my client/friend should have a viewpoint, give input, and make decisions. We then end up with an agreement that becomes his guideline as well as mine. Most frequently, however, the new client is presenting me with a sum of money at the same time I am trying to learn as much as I can about his situation. Incidentally, the most difficult factor for me to understand is usually the psychological background or makeup of the client, which can have an enormous impact on his policy and his resultant asset allocation.

Let me tell you how important I think this subject is. If you happened to be an institution with an enormous amount of money, such as a pension plan, the establishment of a policy that culminates in an asset allocation is probably 85% to 95% of the total investment challenge. For a typical individual, it is probably 50% of the investment challenge. Why the difference? An institution with a very large sum of money cannot easily differentiate itself over a period of time through security selection. Large institutions have so much money to be diversified over such a limited universe of security selections that the asset allocation between fixed income investments and Groups II and III will be the dominant factor in the fund's performance. Individuals with limited sums of money have much more flexibility and can make individual investments that have substantial impacts on their portfolios, including the substantial upside advantage that can be produced by utilizing Group IV investments. As a result, it is my conviction that the establishment of the investment policy and asset allocation for the individual or family is an extremely important part of the investment battle, although it is only half the battle. The selection of securities to implement the policy is the other half.

As a guide for you in establishing your own asset allocation, let me give you what I will call my middle-American model, a reasonably conservative case. You will recognize the scenario from the inflation-hedging contest you have already completed. I have amended that contest only to add a little flesh and blood to the situation and to complicate it by using the four groups of investments we discussed earlier instead of simply fixed income investments versus common stocks. It is hoped you can amend this model to suit your own situation.

This is a family of four with the kids fairly well grown. The father has an occupation with reasonable income prospects, a 20- or 30-year life expectancy, and decent health. The kids are in school, but the income constraints are not overwhelming, because one spouse has a decent, reasonably secure job and the other spouse provides income from a part-time job. Their financial net worth is $100,000, which they have saved. They own their home, which still has a small mortgage at an attractive rate of interest, but they have no other debts. They are not about to inherit a bundle, and they have worked hard to accumulate these savings.

Financially, their characteristics and psychology follow:

- They have never owned many stocks.
- They are conservative, but they are aware of inflation and know that they must look ahead to preserve their purchasing power for retirement.
- They know their fixed income investments are not fighting inflation.
- They conclude that what they really want to do over the next ten years or so is to be as *safe* as possible while protecting their purchasing power. (Remember this challenge?)

With these objectives in mind, I might suggest an investment policy that is reflected in the following asset allocation:

Group I	Fixed income	40%
Group II	Defensive blue-chip common stock	10%
Group III	High-grade growth and blue-chip stocks	50%
Group IV	Aggressive growth or speculative stocks	0%

My reasoning for this asset allocation is that our historical analysis, developed in chapter 8, indicates that we can keep up with inflation if we have 40% to 60% of our assets in high-grade common stocks. We do not need to buy smaller or speculative companies to do this. Our historical background uses the DJIA and the S&P 500, neither of which contains many speculative stocks.

The small percentage invested in Group II reflects the fact that the wild and woolly 1980s left us with few conservative stocks available to buy. Group II stocks are by nature somewhat like surrogates for fixed income investments. To get a feel for this, take a quick look at table 10.1, which compares the Dow Jones Utility Index with the Dow Jones Industrial Average with the Consumer Price Index (CPI), and you can see that hedging inflation with utility stocks would have required an enormous percentage of the portfolio.

I use the middle-American model as a guide and suggest that you tilt these percentages to fit your own situation. If, for example, you have more faith in ownership and common stocks, and your situation permits it, move part of that 40% in fixed income investments down to Groups II, III, and even IV. Change some of my assumptions on the family, and then adjust the asset allocations accordingly. If there is a very strong income need, I might move part of Group III up to Group I. If the family had some confidence in smaller companies, I might have to move part of Group III down to Group IV. As we change the assumptions for the family, we change the asset allocations.

Let me give you a couple of extreme examples from the conservative middle-American model. At one end, a widow with limited assets, a reasonable life expectancy, and a need for maximum income may never get past Group I. As a matter of fact, in a case with limited assets and a strong income need, an old-fashioned annuity may be the most applicable investment. With an annuity, the widow is making a contractual arrangement with an insurance company which, in exchange for a lump-sum investment, agrees to return a set amount of her principal and interest every year for as long as she lives.

At the other extreme is the happy situation of the person with plenty of money, plenty of income, long and successful experience with aggressive investing, and the psychological ability or even proclivity to assume risk and maximize appreciation. In this case, the distribution of assets might look as follows:

Group I   20%
Group II   0%
Group III   40%
Group IV   40%

Some of you more aggressive kids will look at this and say, "Why do we have 20% in the fixed income section if our objective is to go for it?" I will develop my viewpoint a little later on, but a quick answer to your question is that we want to have some money available to buy common stocks when the market goes down.

Now, you try some percentage allocations for yourself. You know the two extremes, a total fixed income orientation or an aggressive posture with 80% in Group III and Group IV. You also have some idea from the conservative model what it takes to fight inflation. Where should you be relative to the model and to the extremes? Think about all your personal qualitative factors. Go back to your balance sheet and see where you are in terms of Groups I through IV. Are you too conservative or too aggressive? In terms of what you know at the moment, put a percentage beside each of the four groups that you think best fits you. If you do all this, and decide where you want to be, you have developed the basics of your investment policy and the resultant asset allocations. Congratulations!

Before I let you go, let me throw out a few further thoughts on your policy. The percentages we established here in these few minutes may be tentative, but the ones you make at the end of the book you should make with conviction. What happens tomorrow and the next day will weaken your resolve. If the market goes up, you

Table 10.1
DJUA/DJIA/CPI (1929–1999)

Year	Dow Jones Utilities Stock Average Close	Dow Jones Industrial Average Close	Consumer Price Index 1982–84 = 100
1929	88.27	248.48	17.2
1930	60.80	164.58	16.1
1931	31.41	77.90	14.6
1932	27.50	59.93	13.1
1933	23.29	99.90	13.1
1934	17.80	104.04	13.4
1935	29.55	144.13	13.8
1936	34.83	179.90	14.0
1937	20.35	120.85	14.4
1938	23.02	154.76	14.0
1939	25.58	150.25	13.9
1940	19.85	131.13	14.1
1941	14.02	110.96	15.5
1942	14.54	119.40	16.9
1943	21.87	135.89	17.4
1944	26.37	152.32	17.8
1945	38.13	192.91	18.2
1946	37.27	177.20	21.5
1947	33.40	181.16	23.4
1948	33.55	177.30	24.1
1949	41.29	200.13	23.6
1950	40.98	235.41	25.0
1951	47.22	269.23	26.5
1952	52.60	291.90	26.7
1953	52.04	289.90	26.9
1954	62.47	404.39	26.7
1955	64.16	488.40	26.8
1956	68.54	499.47	27.6
1957	68.58	435.69	28.4
1958	91.00	583.65	28.9
1959	87.83	679.36	29.4
1960	100.02	615.89	29.8
1961	129.16	731.14	30.0
1962	129.23	652.10	30.4
1963	138.99	762.95	30.9
1964	155.17	874.18	31.2

Table 10.1 *(continued)*

Year	Dow Jones Utilities Stock Average Close	Dow Jones Industrial Average Close	Consumer Price Index 1982–84 = 100
1965	152.63	969.26	31.8
1966	136.18	785.69	32.9
1967	127.91	905.11	33.9
1968	137.17	913.75	35.5
1969	110.08	800.35	37.7
1970	121.84	838.92	39.7
1971	117.75	890.20	41.1
1972	119.50	1020.02	42.5
1973	89.37	850.86	46.2
1974	68.76	616.24	51.9
1975	83.65	852.41	55.5
1976	108.38	1004.65	58.2
1977	111.28	831.17	62.1
1978	98.24	805.01	67.7
1979	106.60	838.74	76.7
1980	114.42	963.99	86.2
1981	109.02	875.00	93.9
1982	119.46	1046.54	97.6
1983	131.84	1258.64	101.3
1984	149.52	1211.57	105.3
1985	174.81	1546.67	109.3
1986	206.01	1895.95	110.5
1987	175.08	1938.83	115.4
1988	186.28	2168.57	120.6
1989	235.04	2753.80	126.1
1990	209.70	2633.66	133.8
1991	226.15	3168.83	137.9
1992	221.02	3301.11	141.9
1993	229.30	3754.09	145.8
1994	181.52	3834.44	149.7
1995	225.40	5117.12	153.5
1996	232.53	6448.27	158.6
1997	273.07	7908.25	161.3
1998	312.30	9181.43	163.9
1999	283.36	11497.12	168.3

will want more stocks, and if it goes down, you will want less. Therefore, I want you to promise yourself that once you have firmly decided what your asset allocation is you will live by it.

Have I implied that we are never allowed to change our approach? I hope not. The second pledge I ask you to make is that if you change your policy, it will be as a product of changes in your own situation and not changes in the outside world. Your policy is a reflection of you, your aims, your situation. If there are dramatic changes in your family, your occupation, your health, etc., you may have to shift your policy equally dramatically. You should promise yourself, however, that external events, such as swings in the stock market, changes in interest rates, war in the Middle East, etc., will not lead you to change your adopted allocations. The biggest mistake I find people making with their asset allocation is to change their percentages as a reflection of the external world and end up selling stocks at the bottom of market swings and buying them at the top. Therefore, I repeat: Your investment policy should fit you, with minor changes, in all seasons, for many years, and should only change as a product of internal changes (changes in your world) and not because of changes in the external world.

•

New Century, Old Approach...

Let's have a moment's review. What we've done thus far is create our balance sheet (where we are in the world), thought about ourselves (begun to build some practical goals), and at least thought about how a conservative and aggressive investor might differ in his or her investment policies. Now we have to create our own policy, and our objective is to have considered ourselves and the investment world enough to allocate our investments by percentages into the four groups we have discussed. Important? You bet. This is half of the investment challenge.

There is a very important difference between the policy approach I am recommending and the approach we see so often in the financial media. Under my approach, when we establish an asset allocation we expect it to be a decision of some permanence, and we expect amendments to it to be made by dramatic changes in individual situations and not by dramatic changes in the outside world. Certainly you have seen recommendations from major firms to increase or decrease the percentage of stocks in your portfolio. I reject this as a forecasting approach that does not relate adequately to you as an individual. If these firms advocate increased stock allocation, it implies that they believe the market will go up, and vice versa. I want to take the forecasting out of it.

Over the last few years, virtually every investment committee with which I work (such as charitable funds) has developed an underlying tone of increasing the stock portion of the portfolio as the market has risen. Every bank and financial institution of which I am aware has increased the stock portion of their suggested allocations over the last decade as the market has risen. Think about it a moment. If the market goes up substantially more than the earnings increase, there presumably exists more risk in stock prices. Yet all these people are essentially advocating that they want to take more and more risk at higher and higher prices! The intellectual case for common stocks obviously grows weaker the higher the market goes. Since we are human beings, however, the emotional affinity for common stocks gets stronger the higher the market goes. At the top of a bull market, most people just love owning stocks. At the top of a bull market, the statistical or intellectual attractiveness of the normal stock on a historical basis is miserable.

I repeat, "The biggest mistake I find people making with their asset allocation is to change their percentages as a reflection of the external world and end up selling stocks at the bottom of market swings and buying them at the top." Promise yourself when you've finished all of this deep thinking and established your asset allocation percentages that you'll live with your decisions. You won't, but if you promise yourself, it might slow down your self-destruction.

CHAPTER 11

Getting Where You Want to Be

IF YOU HAVE GOTTEN THIS FAR, KIDS, YOU ARE DOING GREAT, especially if you completed the exercises. At this point, you should have at least a tentative asset allocation among Groups I through IV, reflecting your financial situation and goals.

The obvious question in implementing your asset allocation is how to deal with the difference between where you are (your current balance sheet) and where you want to be (your brand-new investment policy). Well, the first step, of course, is to compute the amounts of money or values that you want to move from one group to another. If you are currently all Group I, for example, you can compute how much you want to move into each of the other sections. These are your guidelines, and I will try to give you a few thoughts on how you might do this.

As an adjunct to your basic policy, you might, at this point, consider how many different stocks you want to have in a particular group. You are now addressing the question of diversification, a subject that has strong implications for your future performance in much the same fashion as your asset allocation. Assume for the moment that your asset allocation suggests $25,000 in Group I, $15,000 in Group II, $50,000 in Group III, and $10,000 in Group IV, a total of $100,000 in the portfolio. How many different stocks do you want to have? 5? 10? 20? Once you answer this question, you will be able to conclude that a *normal* investment for you in a particular company is a certain amount of money. In the above illustration, for example, you might have 3 investments in Group II, 10 investments in Group III, and 2 investments in Group IV, a total of 15 stocks with a total investment of $75,000. A normal investment for you, therefore, would be approximately $5,000 per company. This is your guideline for the amount to be invested in a stock you like and decide to buy.

From your own balance sheet, I want you to take this step and compute your normal investment per company, but I will give you a few thoughts before you make a decision. The more stocks you have, the more likely you are to act in a fashion coincident with the DJIA and the S&P 500, that is, the more likely you are to act like the market as a whole. The fewer stocks you have, the more likely you are to act in a unique fashion with the impact of your individual securities being greater on your portfolio. Some of the more prominent work in the field of financial economics has centered on this question over the last 20 years, including the three American Nobel Prize winners of 1990. All of us enjoy the concept of reducing risk without giving up potential appreciation, a most difficult exercise. For our purposes, having a few rather simple generalities probably suffices. If hedging inflation is a primary objective, we would probably endorse a rather broad diversification and avoid the risk that our narrow portfolio acts in a contrary fashion to all those DJIA and S&P 500 charts we have studied. It would be a very painful realization in ten years to find that inflation had doubled our cost of living, the DJIA had tripled, and our four or five stocks had not done anything. This is an interesting question for you—to what degree do you *want* to act like the market? If you happen to believe you or your adviser is pretty darn good at stock selections and you can handle the discomfort of wider vicissitudes, you might be willing to assume the risks attendant with having rather few stocks. Using the illustration above, you might have only one Group II investment, three or four Group III investments, and one Group IV investment. In a portfolio like this, you had best make few errors in stock selection.

I frequently use a concept on diversification that might be useful to you if you decide to use Group IV stocks. Recognizing that these investments are substantially more of a risk than the blue chips above, I frequently amend my concept of a normal investment in Group IV to make it somewhat less. For example, in the case I gave, if $5,000 were a normal investment for Group II or Group III, I might regard a normal investment in Group IV for this client to be only $2,500, what we might call one-half of a normal. The hope, of course, is that these stocks will appreciate faster and grow up to be as big as their blue-chip cousins, maybe even become one.

As you address your normal investment question, you might bear in mind the tendency I notice in those of us who are getting older and/or wealthier to build up a larger number of securities in our portfolios whether we mean to or not. Over the years, many of us have bought a few things that have worked pretty well, and we do not want to incur taxes by selling them, even when we find something we like better. When I do my balance sheet every six months, I invariably see a couple of items that I know I would not buy today, but I do not want to sell. Frankly, I am emotionally attached to the companies that have done very well. I also emotionally reject sending tax money to the government. If you were to make the brilliant statement that emotion is the enemy of performance, I would probably agree with you and keep holding those good companies anyway. We older kids have a tendency to have broader butts, bulkier balance sheets (fatter?), and more varied investments.

One of the difficult implementation questions is how rapidly you should try to move from where you are to where you want to be. If the gulf between the two is wide, this can be a rather difficult process. Under certain circumstances, of course, it could be done in a day by using mutual funds to substitute for the four groups with which we work. The personal factors of the individual or family have a great deal to do with how rapidly a substantial change in approach is implemented. With one of my clients, it took me three years to implement her policy and get her where she wanted to be. The portfolio was relatively small, and the situation a very sensitive one, because there was no likelihood of restoring assets if we lost money at the outset. Fortunately, the client was patient. Another problem for me at times is to have enough good stocks to buy to fill an individual portfolio. This is the point at which the investment policy decisions have to meld with the security selection decisions. Frankly, I seldom find I have enough individual companies I want to buy to move very quickly from an all-cash position to a fully invested one if the portfolio is of any size. The exception to the concept of having your buying or selling mode dictate your course of action is when you are basically in a buying mode, but you own a particular stock that you feel is a loser and should be sold. My suggestion is that you go ahead and sell it, recognizing that you are still underinvested in the equity area and that the sale will increase the pressure on you to be in an even stronger buying mode. With this exception, the important idea is to let your asset allocation make you aware of which way you are going and to keep moving in that direction. The question, therefore, of how to fulfill your asset allocation is another subjective judgment to work out with your financial adviser. Generally speaking, I would rather move more slowly than more rapidly.

No matter how substantial the distance between where you are and where your policy tells you to be, and no matter how fast you move to close this gap, the important concept in implementing your policy is that your asset allocation dictates the direction in which you should be aiming. At any one point, aside from the purchase or sale of a particular stock within one of the groups, we will be in one of three modes: buying stocks, selling stocks, or doing nothing. We can use our asset allocation to eliminate either the idea of buying or the idea of selling. If your percentage relationships in your portfolio change and tell you that you should be buying stocks in Group III, you can pretty much scratch the idea of selling and simply concern yourself with when to stop doing nothing and decide what stock you should buy at what price.

I have been talking as if all you kids are sitting on fixed income investments without enough equities. What if you are loaded with stocks and you have decided as a matter of your policy to build up your fixed income section? This can be even tougher since capital gains taxes are frequently involved and you have a real winner that is ten times normal in your portfolio. Once again, knowing you are in a selling mode and having an idea of your normal will be a help. Chances are, every stock you hold is not wonderful; chances are also good that you can do a little shaving on some of your larger holdings to work toward your objective. Take your time and use your judgment.

Putting your plan in place is not always easy, particularly if there is a sizable gap between where you are at the moment and where your investment policy indicates you should be. Your policy itself, however, will give you the first guideline telling you whether you are in a buying or selling mode. The second step is to compute the figure for a normal investment in one company, so you will not be fussing around wondering how much to buy when you or your adviser find something you should buy The third step, deciding how fast to close the gap to get where you want to be, is a judgment call going all the way back to some of those qualitative factors of your particular situation we previously discussed. Follow these steps with care, and, even if it is at a measured pace, you will eventually get where you want to be.

•

Faster Moving World, More Patience...

For most Americans, planning is a lot more difficult than implementation. We Americans like action, and if there is a mountain in view, we want to climb it this morning. This is particularly true in bull markets such as we've had, and particularly with younger common stock buyers. The fact is that implementation of a reasoned investment policy is considerably more difficult today than it was ten years ago, largely because of the bull market and people's expectations of what this can do for them. The number of people who come into my office and essentially say, "I don't have to know what I'm doing, just make me rich, Hunter," has multi-plied substantially.

The few helpful thoughts I expressed ten years ago are still valid, and we might just run over those:

1. Your first step is to quantify the difference between the current asset allocation of your balance sheet and the suggested alloca-tion of your new investment policy.
2. This will create a "mode" for you. You either have to buy or sell some stocks, and you can compute the amount necessary to move from one group to another to fulfill your new policy.
3. Make your diversification decision, how many stocks you want in each group, and consider your normal investment and whether you want to use a smaller amount of money for a stock in your Group IV area.

Now you have an implementation plan.

I find implementing people's policies is more difficult for me than it was ten years ago for several reasons. First among these would be the bull market itself. I have always found it more diffi-cult to find common stocks I want to buy as the market moves up. There is no shortage of attractive companies in the American economy. As a matter of fact, with all the new issues and the avail-ability of information on foreign securities, the number of attrac-tive companies has increased substantially. My problem is price, and it's very difficult for me to pay twice as much for shares in a company relative to the company's earnings and growth rate and all the measurements we use. I've always had the feeling that my plodding approach requires patience on the part of my clients, and in a bull market such as we've had, they are stuck with the fact that I require even more patience. At the same time, because of the bull market, they have less patience.

More frequent today is the problem of the investor with the outsize position in one security that has done very well. There is no magic formula to solve this problem. The only common sense suggestion I can make is to be aware of the percentage in the total portfolio and what kind of exposure it presents to the investor. I could suggest a figure like 10% as a guideline for one company in a sizable portfolio, but a reasonable decision is actually a judgment based on the particular stock and all the personal factors of the investor. Not infrequently in these cases, I manage to make myself even more unpopular with clients by shaving small amounts from their favorite stock over a period of time. If I sell a little of a greatly appreciated stock and it keeps going up, have I made an error? Perhaps one approach to getting where you want to be is to make a long series of minor errors. Incidentally, this is where I am critical of my friend who sold all his stocks two years ago. His policy decision to cut back substantially was well founded, but he should have prohibited himself from forecasting a bad market and instead made a long series of minor errors by selling a bit at a time.

Over the last decade, investors and securities firms have discovered several new questionable ways to implement in a hurry. The growth and popularity of mutual funds have led a great number of investors to go from 20 years of 100% in Group I to 90% in Groups III and IV in a day. This is the reverse of my friend above. Cool it!

Another group comprises mutual fund investors who end up with half a dozen or more funds, owning virtually everything in the world and guaranteeing themselves that their portfolio won't out-perform the market and that they'll have a pretty good tax bill every year.

"Wrap account" clients get pretty spread out when a securities firm has them using three or four managers. They effectively end up with an enormous portfolio in which no particular stock is really going to do them any good.

Patience. Take some time and think about what you're doing, and just keep moving toward the portfolio and asset allocation you want to have.

CHAPTER 12

Making Money

Let's pretend that at this very moment you are *perfect*, an opinion you might want to keep to yourself. You have established your asset allocations, you have implemented your policy by buying or selling some stocks or bonds, and you have ended up exactly where you want to be. Unfortunately, so far you have not made any money. As a matter of fact, you may have spent some with your friendly broker or sent some to Uncle Sam in getting where you want to be, but you certainly have not made any money. Making money is a reasonable aim of investing.

As briefly as I can, and using as little math as possible, I will describe one of the two ways that I find I can make money by investing in stocks over a period of time.

Before I get very far, let me emphasize two important concepts that I try to remember at all times. The first is that I cannot forecast the stock market. I do not know which way it will go, and I do not know anybody who does. The second is that, based upon my asset allocation model, I will be in one of three modes relative to stocks—buying, because my ownership areas are too low; selling, because my ownership areas are too high; or doing nothing. I am very good at doing nothing, as are most of my clients, a point made occasionally by my confreres in the brokerage business.

Let's look at these two points together. When I'm asked what mode I'm in, I'm looking to buy stocks when my fixed income section is too high, not when I think the market is going up. I'm in a selling mode when my common stock percentages are too high, not when I think the market is going down. In this manner, I admit that I do not know what the market will do, but I know what I will do when it changes dramatically either way. I know I will lose some money if the market declines by 30% or 40%, but I also know my asset allocation will put me in a buying mode. Equally important, perhaps, is the fact that it certainly will keep me from selling after the market has declined.

To illustrate these concepts, let's do some pretending. Start by pretending that your portfolio is $100,000 and your asset allocation is very simple: 25% in fixed—good, quiet fixed—and 75% in aggressive common stocks that move 50% faster than the market as a whole (a beta of 1.5). For you, this is *perfect*, you aggressive little monster. I will take you through a series of market movements and show you how your asset allocation model should make you behave and what results you might obtain.

1. We will start by pretending the DJIA is at 2400 and we start off *perfect*, which gives us:

$$\begin{array}{ll} \$ \ 25{,}000 & \text{Fixed (25\%)} \\ + \$ \ 75{,}000 & \text{Stocks (75\%)} \\ \hline \$100{,}000 & \text{Total} \end{array}$$

2. Now we will pretend the DJIA goes from 2400 to 1600, a drop of 33%. Our stocks are not basically better or worse than the market; they simply move faster because of the higher beta, and so we will pretend they go down 50%. On this sad day, our portfolio is as follows:

$$\begin{array}{ll} \$25{,}000 & \text{Fixed (40\%)} \\ + \$37{,}500 & \text{Stocks (60\%)} \\ \hline \$62{,}500 & \text{Total} \end{array}$$

3. At this point, you are discouraged and very unhappy with me, and probably believe the market will go lower—and it might. You will note, however, that your percentage in stocks, because of the decline, is now only 60%. Therefore, your asset allocation tells us we must restore our percentages and put about $9,000 into stocks (getting them back to 75%), much against your will and better judgment. Even worse, you have to raise the $9,000 from Group I, your best-performing group, one endorsed by Ben Franklin, your grandmother, and most Americans. This puts your portfolio as follows:

$16,000 Fixed (25%)
+ $46,500 Stocks (75%)
$62,500 Total

4. Lo and behold, much to our mutual surprise, the market turns around and goes back up to where it started. All the stocks that you have owned also double and go back up to where they started. We will even pretend that every single security in the market went right back to where it started. This assumption will keep you from trying to do this mathematically, which is very frustrating because it requires higher math, well beyond eighth grade, and therefore certainly beyond the scope of both the writer and this book. The lovely fact is you now have a profit on the stocks you bought at the bottom, since they are also fast-moving stocks and they also doubled, giving you a $9,000 profit, from beginning to end, while the DJIA has done nothing. At this point, you are only mildly unhappy with me and your portfolio is as follows:

$ 16,000 Fixed (15%)
+ $ 93,000 Stocks (85%)
$109,000 Total

5. Because your common stocks appreciated as the market returned to our 2400 starting point, you must adjust your percentages again, even though in your mind common stocks are looking a lot better. Therefore, you shift $11,000 to restore your percentage relationships:

$$\begin{array}{ll} \$\ 27,\!000 & \text{Fixed (25\%)} \\ +\ \$\ 82,\!000 & \text{Stocks (75\%)} \\ \hline \$109,\!000 & \text{Total} \end{array}$$

6. This time you are wrong, and the DJIA goes up to 3000. At this point, you are pretty happy with stocks, although you are very unhappy with me again, because I had you do some selling when the market was 2400. Once the DJIA reaches 3000, your fast-moving stocks will give you the following portfolio breakdown:

$$\begin{array}{ll} \$\ 27,\!000 & \text{Fixed (19\%)} \\ +\ \$113,\!000 & \text{Stocks (81\%)} \\ \hline \$140,\!000 & \text{Total} \end{array}$$

The world is bright, but once again you are less than 25% in Group I, which mandates that you be in the selling mode. As much as you like stocks at this point, you do move about $8,000 from the stock section to the fixed income section. Here is where you are:

$$\begin{array}{ll} \$\ 35,\!000 & \text{Fixed (25\%)} \\ +\ \$105,\!000 & \text{Stocks (75\%)} \\ \hline \$140,\!000 & \text{Total} \end{array}$$

7. We will now pretend the DJIA goes back to 2400, right where
   it started in the first place. Your fast-moving stocks go down
   even faster, and you end this up-and-down process as follows:

$$\begin{array}{ll} \$\ 35,000 & \text{Fixed (32\%)} \\ +\ \$\ 75,000 & \text{Equity (68\%)} \\ \hline \$110,000 & \text{Total} \end{array}$$

We will stop there because the DJIA is right where it started and
we have gone both ways. With a total of approximately $110,000,
we have beaten the DJIA by 10%. We made no market forecasts
and even had rather lousy timing on one or two of our transactions. You are still mad at me, but you are richer by 10%.

How often we can augment our performance by moving our
portfolio in this no-brainer fashion, which substitutes mechanics
for forecasting, is very hard to tell. It depends on the movements of
the stock market. The more often and violent the swings in the
DJIA, the better it should work for us. If the DJIA just sits very
steadily or trades within a very narrow range for a protracted
period of time, the less often this approach will work for you. You
can look over tables 8.2 and 8.3 (see pages 86 and 88) showing the
DJIA and the S&P 500 levels over 64 years and get some feel for
what you could expect historically. The more I rely on my asset
allocation model, the more I eliminate psychological and emotional
factors, and the more contrarian I become when I am feeling particularly contrary.

In using this fixed asset allocation approach, conviction is
most necessary at the extremes of market movements. If we get an
extended down market and you have already made one adjustment
by buying stocks, it gets even harder psychologically—and eventually more profitable—to buy more stocks again six or eight
months later when the market is down further. The reverse is true
on the upside. The higher stock prices go, the more people believe
they will continue to go higher. The psychological resistance to
selling becomes stronger.

For me, it is easier to make my adjustments when the market is on its way down, because I am basically an equity-oriented person. Therefore, I enjoy buying stocks more than I like selling stocks. For most people, the reverse is true. They find it harder to buy when the market is down than to sell when the market is up.

This may be an appropriate time to endorse the concept of *dollar cost averaging*, a concept widely advertised by mutual funds, which calls for the investment of fixed amounts of money over a period of time, say $100 a month, that will buy more shares when the market is down and fewer shares when the market is up. If you are using mutual funds to fill your investment policy, this type of program is extremely worthwhile. If you are unfamiliar with the mathematical advantages of it and think it fits you, make one phone call to your friendly investment adviser, who will send you an illustration on virtually any mutual fund you can mention. Generally speaking, I seldom try to dollar cost average with individual common stocks for two reasons: (1) It is difficult to invest smaller fixed sums in individual stocks; and (2) the likelihood of being totally wrong on an individual stock is much greater than it is with a mutual fund. The concept, however, is excellent.

The basic allocation approach I suggest is certainly not my invention. As a matter of fact, back in the 1920s, some prominent institutions tried a somewhat similar approach called *formula planning* with their investments. Most of these early efforts of reacting to the market instead of forecasting it had the problem of reducing the common stock section to zero as the market moved up instead of simply restoring the stock section to an agreed-upon percentage allocation. In other words, those administering the plan decided at a time when the DJIA was at 50, that if it got to 100, they would cut the percentage in stocks from 50% to 25%. Further, if the DJIA ever got as high as 200, they decided in advance that the market would be way too high and the stock section should be eliminated. As a result, many of these institutions were entirely out of the stock market halfway through the Roaring Twenties. They missed a chunk of the bull market, abandoned the formula-planning approach, and paid higher prices to get some of their good stocks back, all just in time to catch the crash of '29.

More recently, however, the approach I am suggesting worked very well in the minicrash of '87. By October 19, Crash Day, the DJIA had lost something like a third of its value in a two-week period. At a point like this, you generally do not have to study your portfolio breakdown to determine that you are under your common stock allocation and therefore in a buying mode. Just for fun a month ago, I looked over my brokerage slips from October 20 and found that I had made 40 purchases and one sale. Apparently, somebody with a normal psyche had called when I was out to lunch (I ain't missin' lunch for no minicrash). There is no question in my mind that the convictions that I could not forecast the market and that asset allocation should be my guide were responsible for the decision to make the purchases and thereby benefit from the market recovery.

For those of you who feel cowed by the institutions, let me just say that they have a tendency to behave just like ordinary people. I am the token broker on the investment policy board of a charitable pension fund. In the mid-1980s, we were fortunate to have a good chairman, who made us take the oath that the normal relationship would be 40% fixed and 60% equities. Unfortunately, by 1987, he had shifted jobs and left town, as most sound bank trust officers do occasionally. In our first two meetings in 1987, our percentage in stocks was over 60% and got to about 70% by our July meeting. The consensus was that we were perhaps a little heavy in stocks, but the world was bright and the outlook was good. Therefore, we did not sell. Well, after the crash, we were only 50% in stocks. At that point, the prevailing view was that our percentage in stocks was perhaps a little low and we should eventually buy more stocks, but this was certainly no time to do anything about it. Therefore, we did not buy. Our committee was forecasting. I remember one guy's comment in response to my urgings to buy: "Deep down, I know you're right, but I just can't do it."

In 1989, when brokers could not find much else to sell to their clients, we had a spate of offerings in *tactical asset allocation funds*.

Outstanding professional managers were to change the makeup of the funds, and the percentages in stocks and bonds and money market funds or whatever were going to be good in the near future, based upon their forecasts of market movements. If the stock market was hot, they were going to have a high percentage of their assets in common stocks, and vice versa with bonds. They varied the percentage relationships instead of restoring them each time to the agreed-upon allocations. Well, by mid-June of 1990, the *Wall Street Journal* published an article pointing out how poorly the "tactical asset allocation funds" had done relative to the market. Apparently, it had not taken much longer than a year to decide that there had to be some better answer to all our prayers than having the experts forecast the stock market's direction.

The toughest question relative to this personalized fixed asset allocation approach is how often we should adjust our portfolio. Unfortunately, no bell goes off and tells you when you should make an adjustment. There is no fixed rule. Obviously, it would be wonderful for both you and your broker if the market were to swing up and down about 50% every month or so, but it won't. In the illustration I used, I made the market swings rather dramatic and also used common stocks with high betas. It is probably a good idea for you to adopt a simple guideline for yourself, perhaps mandating an adjustment in your portfolio when your stock or fixed income sections get as much as 10% out of line. You can make the approach a little fancier by using the percentage relationships, not just between stocks and bonds but between all four groups in your portfolio, if you are using all four groups. The size of your portfolio and other qualitative factors will influence your decision to set points at which your asset allocation should be readjusted. One of the important aspects of the approach, however, is that the wrong bell does not go off on market movements. If nothing else, this system will prevent you from responding to the fear bell when you should be responding to the greed bell.

This system is the only one I know to make an unpredictable stock market work for you. It takes conviction and it takes patience, but I find these to be more easily attainable attributes than the ability to see the future. If you can beat the DJIA by 2% or 3% annually, even with mediocre security selection, you have a pretty good start toward excellent investment performance.

•

Volatile Market, Even More Patience...

If you use the approach I outlined ten years ago, it will work for you over time by producing several results from which most investors almost invariably profit:

1. It will substitute mechanics for emotions.
2. It will force you to sell some stock when prices are high.
3. It will force you to buy some stock when prices are low.

Perhaps as important is to recognize what it won't let you do:

1. It won't let you buy stocks when the market is at a peak.
2. It won't let you sell stocks when the market is in the pits.
3. It will moderate the impact of market fluctuations on the value of your portfolio; and it will thereby not allow you to maximize your gains or your losses over time (I grant you that this could be a negative impact).
4. It will probably reduce your tax payments over time.

The psychological aspects are the difficult part of this approach for the normal investor. We've had such a wonderful stock market for so long that it's simply too confining for many people to stay within their limits. The approach works best in widely fluctuating markets. Since over half of American investors today have not experienced a down market, it will be interesting to see how they respond to their percentage relationships when stocks decline and they are committed to buying stocks by their policy. The mental bulwarks of this approach remain conviction and patience. It requires no advanced brainpower or vision of the future. If it did, I would be forced to abandon it.

CHAPTER 13

Fixed Income Investing

I'M NOT GOING TO TELL YOU EVERYTHING I KNOW ABOUT buying fixed income investments or, to put it another way, lending your money. If I did, this chapter might run three or four pages longer than it does, more than most of you could stand. Briefly, we will face together the challenges of fixed income investing.

Much of the investment world is divided into bond people and stock people. The two meet frequently when they are dealing with portfolios, but otherwise they do not communicate much. I am a stock person, and a good bond person might rightly say that we stock people should not talk about bonds. Except for establishing the policy aspects of a portfolio, I am content to let my bond experts do the specific bond selections in implementing client policies.

Because I am a stock person, I may have a bias against bonds. Generally speaking, I do not think we get paid enough for lending our money. Whether we are talking about U.S. Treasuries or junk bonds, our interest rates both historically and currently have not been high enough to compensate for the risks we assume when we lend. I blame this feeling on the fact that we Americans have been and still are a nation of lenders, who like a good level of income whether we need it or not. You might point out that, in the long term, rates are set by supply and demand. Fine. I just think the suppliers of funds generally do not ask for enough interest from the demanders for funds, considering the risks. Oddly enough, foreign investors also seem to disagree with me. I recently saw some figures on foreign investment in the United States, which showed that foreigners own 21% of our debt securities but only 6% of our equity securities.

As a corollary, I believe that when we do try to get a higher return for lending, we incur even greater than proportionate risks. Junk bonds illustrate the point. Needless to say, as a stock person, I want to take my risks in the ownership section of the portfolio. Also needless to say, I would make a lousy banker—I would make very few loans.

As a framework for this chapter, I will provide my viewpoints on fixed income investing, then give you some historical information, with the understanding that you should amend my approach to build your own fixed income policy. In some ways, the building of the fixed income section of your portfolio is a simple process. The first question to ask yourself is whether taxable bonds, such as U.S. Treasuries, or tax-free bonds, such as municipal bonds, are best suited to your portfolio. The decision as to which of the two types is appropriate for you is based upon your tax situation. A quick way to determine this is to compare the current Treasury yield (taxable) with a high-grade municipal bond (tax free) having a similar maturity, apply your applicable tax rates (use local and state as well as federal taxes in your calculation) to the Treasury yield, and compare the after-tax yield of the two approaches. People in higher tax brackets are almost always beneficiaries of the incremental after-tax return provided by municipal bonds. The degree to which this relative attractiveness of tax-free over taxable bonds exists at any point in time does vary, but it is virtually always in favor of tax-frees for the higher income taxpayer. This is the first step in my approach to constructing your fixed income policy. The remaining conclusions are applicable to either tax-free or taxable bond buyers.

The most important objective in fixed income investing should be the safety of your principal. Losing money in your lending section is an investment sin. An intelligent investor may occasionally speculate on a high return from lending, but these investments should be carried in Groups II, III, or IV, not in Group I. With this objective in mind, I design Group I to produce a reasonable, not a high, rate of return.

Next, the two risks of lending—credit risk and interest rate risk—should be carefully avoided. To do so, the fixed income section (Group I) of my portfolios usually consists of high-grade bonds with reasonably short maturities. The price for avoiding risk is to give up a little income, a price that most investors would be wise to pay. For investors who absolutely require higher levels of income, it is a far-smarter approach to get a reasonable return and consume a measured amount of principal annually than it is to take the risks of producing a higher income and lose a chunk of principal occasionally. For somewhat different reasons, which I will mention shortly, my approach is as applicable to aggressive investors as it is to conservative investors.

Finally, I implement my approach for a large investor by building a *ladder* of maturities and having a reasonably equal number of bonds come due in each of the next several years, no more than ten, giving an average maturity of five years or less, for the bond portfolio. For smaller investors, I recommend a reasonably equal number of bonds, due in two, four, and six years, for example. That's my approach to fixed income investing—and it's set in stone!

Now, let's look at the historical income production or rates of return investors have received on bonds. Just income—no gains, no losses, and no price fluctuations. In the first column of table 13.1, you will see the annual income return for a group of high-grade corporate bonds in each year since 1950. These figures are based on Standard & Poor's Corporate Bond Index. They are good quality bonds, AA ratings or better, with maturities averaging 20 years. These bonds are taxable and have historically paid more than the equivalent maturities in U.S. Treasuries, simply because AA corporate bonds have to return more than Treasuries to attract investors. You can see that the average return of these bonds has been close to 7% over the years.

Since I must pay taxes on these bonds before I spend the income, I computed an adjustment to the rate of return by assuming that this investor had to pay one-third of his income to federal, state, and local governments annually. Therefore, the second column on table 13.1 is the annual return after taxes for this investor. I should mention that if I were using municipal bonds instead of these taxable corporate bonds for the high-tax-bracket investor, the result in this column would be a little bit better than the 4.658% return that it shows, maybe 1% better. I also might point out that if your tax bracket is considerably less than my assumption, these taxable bonds would accordingly be more attractive to you.

Stay with me. As you might have guessed, the most disturbing factor in lending is that old bugaboo, inflation. Therefore, I included the third column of table 13.1, showing the inflation rate during each of these years, so you could compare it with the after-tax income figure in the second column. Finally, in the last column, I computed the after-tax and after-inflation return produced in each year. You knew I would.

You can draw some rather frightening conclusions from this table, the first being the fact that the average net annual income from 1950 through 1990 using this investment approach came to approximately one-third of 1% in real dollars! Wow! Another conclusion is that you would have had to save virtually all your income if you were using lending as a means of trying to protect your purchasing power. That is a tough one to swallow, since we lend our money to receive income and would not be allowed to spend any of it. A corollary would be that virtually everything we spend out of this income is in one sense a consumption of our purchasing power principal. In any event, you would have to be a whale of a saver to get rich by lending.

Remember that, in table 13.1, I excluded price fluctuations on your principal and tried to look only at income from lending. Now, let's bring in the impact of market price changes. In table 13.2, in the second column, you will see the annual return in each year since 1926, which includes both income and appreciation or depreciation,

Table 13.1

Annual Income Return
High-Grade Corporate Bonds vs. Inflation

Year	Annual Income High-Grade Corporate Bonds	Annual Income Tax-Effected Corporate Bonds	Inflation Rate	After-Tax & Inflation Real Return
1950	2.6%	1.73%	5.8%	−4.07%
1951	3.1	2.07	5.9	−3.83
1952	3.0	2.00	0.9	1.10
1953	3.1	2.07	0.6	1.47
1954	2.9	1.93	−0.5	2.43
1955	3.1	2.07	0.4	1.67
1956	3.4	2.27	2.9	−0.63
1957	3.7	2.47	3.0	−0.53
1958	4.1	2.73	1.8	0.93
1959	4.6	3.07	1.5	1.57
1960	4.4	2.93	1.5	1.43
1961	4.4	2.93	0.7	2.23
1962	4.2	2.80	1.2	1.60
1963	4.4	2.93	1.6	1.33
1964	4.4	2.93	1.2	1.73
1965	4.7	3.13	1.9	1.23
1966	5.3	3.54	3.4	0.14
1967	6.9	4.60	3.0	1.60
1968	6.5	4.34	4.7	−0.36
1969	7.8	5.20	6.1	−0.90
1970	7.4	4.94	5.5	−0.56
1971	7.1	4.74	3.4	1.34
1972	7.2	4.80	3.4	1.40
1973	7.7	5.14	8.8	−3.66
1974	8.6	5.74	12.2	−6.46
1975	8.6	5.74	7.0	−1.26
1976	7.8	5.20	4.8	0.40
1977	8.4	5.60	6.8	−1.20
1978	9.2	6.14	9.0	−2.86
1979	10.6	7.07	13.3	−6.23

Table 13.1 *(continued)*

Annual Income Return
High-Grade Corporate Bonds vs. Inflation

Year	Annual Income High-Grade Corporate Bonds	Annual Income Tax-Effected Corporate Bonds	Inflation Rate	After-Tax & Inflation Real Return
1980	12.4%	8.27%	12.4%	−4.13%
1981	14.5	9.67	8.9	0.77
1982	11.2	7.47	3.9	3.57
1983	12.3	8.20	3.8	4.40
1984	12.0	8.00	4.0	4.00
1985	10.1	6.74	3.8	2.94
1986	9.1	6.07	1.1	4.97
1987	9.9	6.60	4.4	2.20
1988	9.9	6.60	4.4	2.20
1989	8.8	5.87	4.6	1.27
1990	9.1	6.07	6.1	0.03
1991	8.5	5.61	3.1	2.51
1992	8.3	5.48	2.9	2.48
1993	7.3	4.82	2.7	2.12
1994	8.5	5.61	2.7	2.91
1995	6.8	4.49	2.5	1.99
1996	7.4	4.88	3.3	1.58
1997	6.9	4.55	1.6	2.85
1998	6.8	4.49	1.6	2.89
1999	6.7	4.42	2.7	1.72
Average	**7.1%**	**4.70%**	**3.9%**	**.77%**

Table 13.2

Stocks, Bonds, and Inflation

(Annual Percentage Return Including Income)

Year	S&P 500	Long-Term Government Bonds	Consumer Price Index
1926	11.6%	7.8%	− 1.5%
1927	37.5	8.9	− 2.0
1928	43.6	0.1	− 1.0
1929	− 8.4	3.4	0.2
1930	−24.9	4.7	− 6.1
1931	−43.3	− 5.3	− 9.5
1932	− 8.1	16.9	−10.3
1933	53.9	− 0.1	0.5
1934	− 1.4	10.0	2.0
1935	47.6	5.0	2.9
1936	34.0	7.5	1.2
1937	−35.0	0.2	3.1
1938	31.1	5.5	− 2.7
1939	− 0.4	6.0	− 0.5
1940	− 9.8	6.1	1.0
1941	−11.6	0.9	9.7
1942	20.3	3.2	9.3
1943	25.9	2.1	3.2
1944	19.7	2.9	2.2
1945	36.4	10.7	2.2
1946	− 8.1	− 0.1	18.1
1947	5.5	− 1.9	9.0
1948	5.4	3.6	2.8
1949	17.8	5.8	− 1.9
1950	30.5	− 0.8	5.8
1951	23.4	− 1.5	5.9
1952	17.7	2.3	0.9
1953	− 1.2	3.8	0.6
1954	51.2	4.2	− 0.5
1955	31.0	− 1.3	0.3
1956	6.4	− 3.2	2.9
1957	−10.5	8.1	3.1
1958	42.4	− 5.9	1.8
1959	11.8	− 4.0	1.5
1960	0.3	14.6	1.5
1961	26.6	− 0.9	0.7
1962	− 8.8	7.0	1.3
1963	22.5	0.4	1.7
1964	16.3	4.2	1.2
1965	12.3	0.9	2.0

Table 13.2 *(continued)*

Stocks, Bonds, and Inflation

(Annual Percentage Return Including Income)

Year	S&P 500	Long-Term Government Bonds	Consumer Price Index
1966	−10.0%	2.6%	3.3%
1967	23.7	− 4.4	3.1
1968	10.8	1.4	4.7
1969	− 8.3	− 5.5	6.1
1970	3.5	13.7	5.5
1971	14.1	13.1	3.3
1972	18.7	6.2	3.4
1973	−14.5	0.7	8.8
1974	−26.0	− 0.2	12.2
1975	36.9	9.1	7.0
1976	23.6	16.6	4.8
1977	− 7.2	2.9	6.8
1978	6.4	− 4.2	9.0
1979	18.2	− 3.0	13.3
1980	31.5	− 4.9	12.4
1981	− 4.9	− 1.3	8.9
1982	20.4	43.4	3.9
1983	22.3	5.2	3.9
1984	6.0	9.2	4.0
1985	31.1	31.8	3.8
1986	18.5	24.1	1.1
1987	5.7	− 4.2	4.4
1988	16.3	8.5	4.4
1989	31.2	19.3	4.6
1990	− 3.1	5.2	6.1
1991	30.0	17.2	3.1
1992	7.4	8.0	2.9
1993	9.9	17.3	2.7
1994	1.3	− 6.9	2.7
1995	37.1	30.7	2.5
1996	22.7	− 0.8	3.3
1997	33.1	10.4	1.7
1998	28.3	15.0	1.6
1999	20.9	−11.5	2.7
Average	**13.1%**	**5.4%**	**3.2%**

for the same kind of corporate bonds we were looking at in the previous example, before tax and before inflation. For those of you who like looking at these tables, you can see that column three gives the annual percentage return, including income, for government bonds, and column four shows short-term Treasury bills. I might say that these figures are largely supported by extensive and authoritative studies done by various research firms over the years. If you spend a little time with table 13.2, I think you will agree that the aura of stability for bonds that comes from looking at the income-only table (table 13.1) dissipates when we see the annual price fluctuations of long-term bonds. These tables should impress upon you the fact that there is plenty of risk in buying even high-quality, long-term bonds.

It will not surprise me if you consider my comments of caution to be a bit extreme. We Americans have a tendency to believe that what is happening at the moment will continue, and our current thinking is colored by the fact that the 1980s were a benevolent period for bond investors because interest rates and the inflation rate declined from historically high levels. The inflation rate over the last decade dropped to almost one-third of its previously double-digit levels, and interest rates gradually declined through most of the decade. Thus, these years were the best possible time to be investing in bonds. It would be a little optimistic to forecast the 1990s as a period in which we can produce the same levels of lending results we enjoyed recently because interest rates are at such low historical levels that it will be difficult to improve upon them.

Many years ago a popular investment policy concept was that investors should go from common stocks into long-term bonds when they believed the stock market was too high. My contention is that you should move somewhat from the stock market to short-term, high-grade bonds when your portfolio tells you the stock market is high. Notice the two differences. I am not forecasting the market; I am using my portfolio guidelines and I am certainly not going from common stocks to long-term bonds. The year 1969 provided a good lesson to the practitioners of the old theory. The

DJIA was near 1000 at the end of 1968, and I can remember a few seasoned sages shifting their portfolios from corporate stocks to corporate bonds. Well, they were half-right. The stock market declined sharply in 1969, but so did corporate bonds. Bondholders received 7.8% in income but lost over 15% of their principal in 1969 as inflation accelerated. A period of rising inflation is generally not very healthy for stocks, but it is certainly very unhealthy for bonds.

Now that we see clearly what wonderful rates of return we get from lending, let's return to those two lending risks I mentioned way back in chapter 4—credit risk and interest rate risk. Credit risk, the risk that we will not be paid our principal and interest, is well recognized by Americans and easy to avoid. One easy way to avoid it, of course, is to lend our money so that it is guaranteed by the federal government, which has spent the last decade or so guaranteeing every financial institution in the nation at the expense of the next generation. The second easy way to avoid credit risk, and one I recommend you watch carefully, is to refer to the rating agencies and keep your lendings in the AA or AAA categories. Generally speaking, either of these approaches will avoid credit risk. I might add that another point in favor of short maturity bonds is that institutions in today's world often move from a AAA to a BBB in a rather short period of time. A short maturity offers some defense against a deteriorating credit.

The second risk—interest rate risk—is that the value of your bonds will decline as interest rates move up. The degree of this risk is ignored by many Americans who feel they have a *safe* bond because it is of high quality. Table 13.3 demonstrates how much the market value of your bond will drop as interest rates increase. For example, an 8%, 15-year bond will lose 8.1% of its value if interest rates rise by 1%, and from the second table we can see that the same 8%, 15-year bond will lose 15.4% of its value if interest rates increase by 2%. This happens as the market price of your bonds adjusts to the changes in interest rates. The next time you think of buying a long-term bond, even of the highest quality, pull out this chart and ask yourself whether the degree of risk you are

Table 13.3
Interest Rates and Bond Prices

1. Price changes for bonds when interest rates rise or fall by one percentage point

Years to Maturity	4% Coupon If Rates		6% Coupon If Rates		8% Coupon If Rates		10% Coupon If Rates	
	RISE	FALL	RISE	FALL	RISE	FALL	RISE	FALL
1	− 1.0%	+ 1.0%	− 1.0%	+ 1.0%	− 0.9%	+ 1.0%	−0.9%	+ 0.9%
2	− 1.9	+ 1.9	− 1.8	+ 1.9	− 1.8	+ 1.8	−1.8	+ 1.8
3	− 2.8	+ 2.9	− 2.7	+ 2.8	− 2.6	+ 2.7	−2.7	+ 2.6
4	− 3.6	+ 3.7	− 3.4	+ 3.6	− 3.3	+ 3.4	−3.2	+ 3.3
5	− 4.4	+ 4.6	− 4.2	+ 4.4	− 4.0	+ 4.2	−3.8	+ 4.0
10	− 7.8	+ 8.6	− 7.1	+ 7.8	− 6.5	+ 7.1	−6.0	+ 6.5
15	−10.5	+12.0	− 9.2	+10.5	− 8.1	+ 9.2	−7.3	+ 8.1
20	−12.6	+15.0	−10.7	+12.6	− 9.2	+10.7	−8.0	+ 9.2
30	−15.5	+19.7	−12.5	+15.5	−10.3	+12.5	−8.7	+10.3

2. Price changes for bonds when interest rates rise or fall by two percentage points

Years to Maturity	4% Coupon If Rates		6% Coupon If Rates		8% Coupon If Rates		10% Coupon If Rates	
	RISE	FALL	RISE	FALL	RISE	FALL	RISE	FALL
1	− 1.9%	+ 2.0%	− 1.9%	+ 1.9%	− 1.9%	+ 1.9%	− 1.8%	+ 1.9%
2	− 3.7	+ 3.9	− 3.6	+ 3.8	− 3.6	+ 3.7	− 3.5	+ 3.6
3	− 5.4	+ 5.8	− 5.2	+ 5.6	− 5.1	+ 5.4	− 4.9	+ 5.2
4	− 7.0	+ 7.7	− 6.7	+ 7.3	− 6.5	+ 7.0	− 6.2	+ 6.7
5	− 8.5	+ 9.5	− 8.1	+ 9.0	− 7.7	+ 8.5	− 7.4	+ 8.1
10	− 14.9	+ 18.1	− 13.6	+ 16.5	− 12.5	+ 14.9	− 11.5	+ 13.6
15	− 19.6	+ 25.8	− 17.3	+ 22.4	− 15.4	+ 19.6	− 13.8	+ 17.3
20	− 23.1	+ 32.8	− 19.8	+ 27.4	− 18.9	+ 27.7	− 16.2	+ 22.6
30	− 27.7	+ 45.0	− 22.6	+ 34.8	− 18.9	+ 27.7	− 16.2	+ 22.6

3. Price changes for bonds when interest rates rise or fall by four percentage points

Years to Maturity	4% Coupon If Rates		6% Coupon If Rates		8% Coupon If Rates		10% Coupon If Rates	
	RISE	FALL	RISE	FALL	RISE	FALL	RISE	FALL
1	− 3.8%	N/A	− 3.7%	+ 3.9%	− 3.7%	+ 3.9%	− 3.6%	+ 3.8%
2	− 7.3	N/A	− 7.1	+ 7.8	− 6.9	+ 7.6	− 6.8	+ 7.4
3	−10.5	N/A	−10.2	+11.6	− 9.8	+11.2	− 9.5	+10.8
4	−13.5	N/A	−12.9	+15.3	−12.4	+14.7	−11.9	+14.0
5	−16.2	N/A	−15.4	+18.9	−14.7	+18.0	−14.1	+17.1
10	−27.2	N/A	−24.9	+36.1	−22.9	+32.7	−21.2	+29.8
15	−34.6	N/A	−30.8	+51.6	−27.5	+44.8	−24.8	+39.2
20	−39.6	N/A	−34.2	+65.7	−30.1	+54.7	−26.7	+46.2
30	−45.3	N/A	−37.9	+89.8	−32.3	+69.5	−28.1	+55.4

N/A = Not applicable

Sources: *Journal of the American Association of Individual Investors* and First Albany Corporation.

assuming is offset by the incremental return you will receive. One bad year in the bond market can take away your incremental return for years to come.

Now, you might point out how much your bond can *appreciate* when interest rates come down. Unfortunately, bond buying is not fully a two-way street, because most bonds clearly state that the bond can be redeemed (called) by the issuer at a price near par. If interest rates come down, you have a pretty good chance of having that good-looking bond refinanced or called. Therefore, you get a little bit of the profit and the problem of reinvesting at lower rates of return. I point this out not to discourage you from buying bonds with nearby call features. I am simply recommending that you have the call features in mind when you are buying a bond and calculate the yield to call as well as yield to maturity. Try to buy bonds with which you will be happy if they are called and even happier if they are not.

The important message here, however, is how much the market value of your principal can be eroded by an increase in interest rates. In smaller portfolios, therefore, I try to build a ladder of maturities in the two- to seven-year range, and, in large portfolios, I seldom go beyond ten-year maturities. In a larger account, if I have some bonds coming due in each of the next ten years, my average maturity will only be about five years, certainly a tolerable risk for a sizable portfolio.

Despite my preaching, many of you are not going to want your lendings to be both high grade and short in maturity. You are going to want to take advantage of your guess/forecast that interest rates will come down and therefore *lock-in* what seem to be high rates of return. My suggestion is that when you do assume these incremental risks, take the bond out of Group I in your portfolio and move it down to Group II. If you buy a low-quality, long bond, I suggest you move it even further down to Group III or even Group IV, since it can have a fluctuation every bit as great as a stock. A junk bond, for example, which you may think is attractive as a speculation because of its inordinately high rate of return, you might take all the way down to Group IV, where you have your aggressive stocks. Even as a stock person, I feel these temptations at points of high interest rates and low bond prices. As a stock person, however, I also find that during these same periods, common stocks are also down, and I end up buying a stock instead.

Their vague understanding of these lending risks leads Americans to adopt some dubious fixed income investing practices. One practice is to use municipal bond mutual funds to produce a high rate of return and still be *safe*. Before you buy a municipal bond fund, take a look at the maturities of the bonds in that fund and recognize that interest rate risk is not eliminated by having 100 long bonds instead of 1 or 2. Incidentally, you might also take a look at the costs and fees of using this approach. A second error made by a great number of older people is to try to replace the high income from a maturing bond at a point when interest rates are low. Sure enough, to retain the income levels, they either stretch the maturities or reduce the quality of their bond. Do not do it. A third practice of many bond investors has been wonderful for brokerage firms. For some number of years during periods of rising interest rates, almost annually in November and December, investors would *swap* their municipal bonds and incur losses to offset their common stock gains. Seldom was this done to avoid risk. Over a period of time, this is almost a sure way to reduce the effectiveness of the fixed income section of your portfolio. I remember calling this practice "the broker's reward for being wrong in the first place."

After mentioning all these worrisome aspects of fixed income investing, you might assume that I use few bonds in portfolios. Quite the opposite. I use fixed income investments in virtually all my portfolios, and most of these are bonds in one form or another. For conservative investors who absolutely need high current income, bonds can at least provide a measured and higher current return on our investment than common stocks. Second, some of us conservative kids have reached an age where we do not necessarily try to keep up with inflation, let alone beat it. These worrisome aspects of bonds are more easily avoided than the worrisome aspects of common stocks. It is simply a matter of tailoring the investment policy to fit the individual.

If your fixed income policy should be centered, as I suggest, on high-grade bonds with short maturities, what does this mean to the aggressive investor who wants to increase his wealth? In the previous chapter, I described the only way I know to make money from fluctuations in the stock market—having my asset allocation dictate the purchase of common stocks (Groups II, III, and IV) when the stock market goes down and I have lost money in stocks. Now, to do this successfully, the Group I section of my portfolio must be stable. If I take substantial risks in my lendings, there is every likelihood that the value of my bond section (Group I) will decline almost as far as my common stocks during an adverse period. Therefore, in a difficult time, with an aggressive Group I, I am losing money throughout my portfolio, not just in the equity section, and there is not enough percentage change in the different groups for me to reallocate my assets. They are all lower. As an aggressive investor, therefore, I want my Group I investments to be my harbor from stormy seas and a source of funds when my common stocks decline substantially. This is the strongest reason I know for the aggressive investor to adopt a conservative fixed income policy, keeping his maturities short and his quality high. He wants the price stability and the resultant liquidity for the opportunity periods in the stock market.

I find that a good many people to whom municipal bonds are applicable have a distrust or lack of understanding of the municipal market that prevents them from investing as well as they could. Certainly, if we are buying reasonably short-term bonds, the Standard & Poor's and Moody ratings of AA and AAA can give you comfort. I might observe that the market for municipal bonds in many states, including Pennsylvania, is not necessarily a very efficient one. Therefore, if you have a good bond adviser, you can occasionally take advantage of incremental returns without incurring incremental risks. Bonds selling at substantial discounts or premiums frequently offer a somewhat better return than bonds selling at par. Banks are a major force in most municipal markets. They have an affinity for bonds selling at or near par if for no other reason than to avoid explaining to their clients why they are not getting much return on their discount bonds or how they are *losing* part of their principal by buying premium bonds (they are getting their principal back from the high return while they hold the bond). The fact is that either discount or premium bonds can be more attractive than bonds selling at par. Some years ago, I had a good friend who was a whiz on Pennsylvania municipal bonds. We would, of course, debate the merits of stocks versus bonds, which led to no change in either position, the normal outcome of most investing debates. We lived in an inflationary world, but he was so good at buying bonds in that inefficient market that he almost made up for it. If you do not have a friend with these capabilities, stick to the ratings as your quality guidelines. With good quality and short maturities, you will keep your Group I stable and have funds readily available for buying in a down stock market.

I have a suspicion that the material I have presented to you on bond returns and risks is a little disheartening, one of those bothersome concepts of which we are vaguely aware but would rather not face. As a result, almost all of us have been tempted from time to time by the brokerage ads in the Sunday papers—the ones with stars beside what looks like a very good rate of return. The ad may even describe these bonds as *guaranteed* by some entity or even by the federal government. Well, every time you get tempted to buy either a long bond or a lower-quality bond, just sit down and figure out how much the incremental after-tax return will affect your standard of living. If you perform this little calculation, you might save yourself a few worrisome moments in your fixed income investing.

•

New Century, Same Old Approach...

The last decade has simply fortified my conservative convictions. Fixed income investing should be done in a conservative fashion by virtually all conservative investors and almost all aggressive investors. I am surprised how few objections I've had to my approach over the years, particularly from those whom I call "bond people." As a stock person, I have retained my prejudice against long-term bonds with the generality that we are not paid enough in this country for lending our money. We should be paid more for the risks we assume. As a stock person, I want to take my risks in common stocks, not bonds.

I concentrated in my comments on the two primary risks, interest rate risk and credit risk. I haven't done so, but I guess we could add consideration of foreign bonds to today's world.

A new set of risks: political risk. Are Canadians foreign? I have to tell you about one audience member at a talk I gave in Jasper, Canada. I had told the audience that they could hold their hands up, ask questions, and express their viewpoints without fear of interrupting a deep train of thought while I was talking. I then proceeded to tell them, in my endearing fashion, that I thought Canadians were really pretty dumb. They had all this beautiful land, great resources, and a small population base, but they voted themselves such expensive social programs that they had every likelihood of being broke forever. This guy's hand went up, and, as I'd promised, I recognized him. He said, "You don't understand, Hunter. We know we can't afford those programs, but we have these neighbors to the south of us who lend us all the money to pay for them. They're the ones who are really dumb."

The aggressive investor should particularly want his bonds to be high grade and short term, so the values are stable and funds are readily available for down markets. The conservative investor keeps his bonds high grade and short term because he is conservative and doesn't want to lose his money. He has a better case for somewhat longer maturities.

In table 13.3, I showed the amount of principal lost to the bond owner in the market as interest rates rose. I don't think people spend enough time with this table, so I will reduce the coupon to 6% to reflect more current rates and simply show you again your risk to principal in a bond market of rising interest rates.

I noticed that in chapter 13 I made the same forecast on bonds that I made on stocks. I said that the 1980s were a benevolent period for bond investors because both interest rates and inflation rates declined. Therefore, it seemed unlikely to me that the 1990s would be as benevolent to bonds as the 1980s had been. Wrong again.

Even in a good decade, however, bond investors in 1994 again learned how much of their principal they could lose in a short period of time.

My summary on bonds:

1. Decide whether you should buy taxable or tax-free bonds.
2. Reduce your risk by buying short-term, high-grade bonds.
3. Build a ladder of maturities going no more than ten years, even if you have a bushel of money. If you have only a peck of money, keep your maturities shorter.
4. If you do buy a long-term, low-quality bond, as a speculation on a high return, take it out of Group I and put it in Group II, III, or IV.

CHAPTER 14

Common Stock Investing

ANYTIME ANYBODY TALKS ABOUT THE *FACTS* OF COMMON stock investing, they should confess that it is only their opinion—especially me. But, it is a fact that common stock investing is, for me, the most challenging aspect of investing. Everything we've talked about up to this point is relatively pedestrian. I hope the book so far contains a bit of common sense, a viewpoint of history, and a smidgen of logic. Even in fixed income investing, my major thrust is low key: prevent errors, play defense, don't get beat up lending your money. The primary goal of common stock investing, however, is to play offense, to make money. As I said before, for the individual investor, this business of common stock selection can be as much as 50% of the investment and intellectual challenge, so if there is any section of this book that should be fun, this is it.

Because my focus in this book is primarily on investment policy, not individual common stock selection, in this chapter I will confine myself to those areas of stock selection that are most meaningful in terms of policy. I will discuss first general concepts applicable to all common stock investing and then address each of the three groups into which I divide the common stock world. I hope you can fit this approach to yourself and gain some insight as to how to implement your own investment policy.

GENERAL COMMON STOCK CONCEPTS

I frequently use modern art appreciation as an analogy to common stock selection. It is an easy analogy for me, since I know nothing about modern art. If 20 of us clods took an introductory course in modern art appreciation, the teacher would presumably give us some guidelines and explain the techniques the artists used. Likewise, an introductory course in securities analysis would explain how to use such tools as cash flow, price-earnings (P-E) ratios, yields, book values, and growth rates. If we worked hard, even those of us students with little skill would pass the art course. Certainly, those with ninth-grade math skills willing to apply themselves could pass the equivalent securities analysis course. After the art course, if the teacher took us to the annual Carnegie International modern art exhibit, I believe only one, two, or perhaps none of the class would be able to look at a particular painting, say it's terrific, and somehow know it truly is. There is a vast difference between learning the mechanics of analysis and being able to recognize greatness. The same is true in common stock selection, and one's ability to make good stock selections is largely indiscernible at the outset, even if the numerical analysis has been properly performed. Over the years, gifted students will find, perhaps to their own surprise, that they are often correct in their selections. Securities selection is not an art. It's *art appreciation*. The art is the company itself, just as the picture at the Carnegie is the art. The stock picker recognizes the art, prices it, and tries to extend its value into the future.

Much has been said about the impact of computers on the business of security selection, using quantitative analysis to select securities. I regard the computer as helpful, but in the long term and at the critical points, quantitative analysis alone will not do the job. Good stock selection over time is more qualitative and subjective, a liberal arts rather than a mathematical exercise.

A few years ago, I was invited to listen to the head of a major research firm, which had invested enormous sums in computer research. He probably does not remember saying this, but his comment was: "Life is a discounted cash flow analysis." I laughed. Even applying the phrase to a single stock, let alone life itself, is a little heady for me. Sometimes I think we have spent so much money on computers that we *have* to use them. I am reminded of the old saw about giving a four-year-old a hammer—he begins to think everything in the house is a nail. The computer is able to do mountains of mechanical work, and for that it is very helpful. Perhaps it could be programmed to pass introductory art appreciation, but it has not yet been invited to be a judge at the Carnegie art exhibit.

When you buy stock in a particular company, it is helpful to recognize the two influences on your stock's price performance while you own it. One will be the gyrations of the stock market; the second will be the results of the company. As a rule of thumb, I would say the stock market will have the greater influence on the stock price in the short term, and the results of the company will have the greater influence on the stock price in the long term.

The fact that there will be two influences on the price of a stock you own is an important concept to keep in mind. I fervently believe that no one can forecast the short-term stock market. Even today, this is to some people the most disturbing, heretical, and debatable concept I mention in this book. I say *short term* because I am among those who feel the stock market will have an upward movement over an extended period of time, from the gradual growth of American businesses, if nothing else. That is about as much as I will forecast. Of all the people I have known who have done extremely well investing in common stocks, no one had a short-term market forecast as their focal approach. As a matter of fact, I believe that any success from market forecasting comes from being a contrarian, not a member of the majority. Years ago, economists concluded their year-end speeches about the economy with a market forecast—the part that everybody really came to hear. However, the forecasts were so bad that they impinged on the credibility of the economists' basic work. As a result, they all stopped doing the market forecast (and, therefore, lost a chunk of their audience).

Twenty-five years ago, my belief was a lot more heretical than it is today. If you read the savants of security analysis today, you will find very few if any articles on how to predict the stock market. Those of you who have been around for a while might see the same trend in our daily business reading material, like the *Wall Street Journal*, where, in the short term, the dart throwers outperform the professional stock pickers frequently. The only people I know who have profited handsomely by forecasting the stock market are those who write market forecast letters and sell them for $200 a year to pigeons across the nation.

The fact that we do not know where the market is going does not eliminate some useful market information. We are allowed to know whether stocks are historically high or historically low and whether P-E ratios are historically high or historically low. We are allowed to know where the market is at the moment and where it has been. Fortunately, the conviction that we do not know which way it will go allows us to make our asset allocation approach work better. We are allowed to know what we will do, buy or sell, when the market does whatever it is going to do. I find that telling yourself what you will do far in advance helps you psychologically to act when the market has dropped or risen substantially. I know right now that if the market drops 25% in the next six months, I will be buying what I hope are temporarily wilted flowers at lower prices.

I only know three groups of people who do extremely well in common stock investing, and two of these groups are not very big. The first group consists of those few people who generally own one stock, usually because they work for the company, and the company does very well over a period of time. They hold the stock because it is their company, they show their loyalty by holding the stock, or maybe they do not even know they can sell it. You could call this a no-brainer approach, but some of them love that stock, and, in some cases, they should.

This is an appropriate time for an additional word about diversification. One of the hackneyed expressions in the securities business is "You should not have all your eggs in one basket." Try telling that to a guy who has made $50 million on his stock in a small computer company. As I previously mentioned, I believe diversification should stem from the aims of the individual investor, but there is also a point to be made from the experience of these people who made a bundle on one stock. It is simply that they allowed themselves to do it. The one-stock holders had the faith and perseverance to allow a winner to really win by not selling it. Too many of us sell a stock too soon and do not permit it to make us enough money over time by becoming a great company. In North Carolina 20 or so years ago, a few neighbors invested in a small supermarket chain, which became very successful. A bunch of them held on because they knew the company and the management. One of these investors sold when his profits bought him a new riding lawn mower. It is now colloquially known as the *$3 million lawn mower*. I understand it is still working well.

The second group of winners is the largest. It is all the people across the country who try to select stocks in good companies and do not shift around very much. They let the good companies work and grow. Some of these people will occasionally sell a stock when they do not think it is going to do very well or buy one when they think it will do well. Over a period of time, they have differing results, but they are successful investors. Most of these people own common stocks through both good and bad times in the market. What differentiates people in this group from each other in terms of their investment performance is frequently the long-term results of the companies they own. Some of them, however, consistently own better stocks than other people, and you should try to be among them.

This leads me to the *growth-stock theory*, the most commonly accepted approach to producing good common stock investment results over a period of time, and the one that I heartily endorse. This theory concentrates on buying companies with sales and earnings that generally increase at better than an average rate. Those of us who endorse the growth-stock theory are concentrating on cash flow and earnings per share, both now and in the future, for the company we buy. We, therefore, study companies in the belief that the future earnings results of these companies are somewhat forecastable even if the overall stock market is not. Years ago, David L. Babson did a very simple little study contrasting ten popular income stocks with ten popular growth stocks. Forgetting about the price appreciation from the growth stocks versus the others, the study showed that, by the end of ten years, the growth stocks were actually producing more in dividends than the income stocks. I liked that little study. The work we do studying a particular growth stock is focused on the question of future earnings. We learn as much as we can about the company and decide what we think this year's earnings will be, what next year's earnings will be, and how likely it is that earnings will continue to trend upward in future years.

Unfortunately, the work we do in studying a company and forecasting earnings does not eliminate the element of risk that comes from fluctuations in the market itself. Take another minute with tables 8.2 and 8.3 (see pages 86 and 88), which show the price performance of the Dow Jones and S&P 500 averages over the years. The earnings over the last decade, if you will recall, increased rather nicely, but not nearly as nicely as the averages themselves. You will notice again that the P-E ratio for the Dow closed at over 15 times earnings in 1990, double what it was ten years earlier. As I write, we have had a pleasant stock market in 1991, and this average is currently in the area of 20 times estimated earnings. Obviously, this has been a favorable stock market environment for shareholders, and, almost equally obviously, it can go the other way. The growth-stock investor, therefore, is hoping to find a company that will increase its earnings substantially in a reasonably short period of time and that the market influence on the stock will not be strongly negative. If I can buy stock in a company that grows its earnings at 20% a year, I will double my money in 3.6 years (the rule of 72) as long as there is no change in the P-E ratio. Of course, growth-stock purchasers would like to be right on their earnings forecast and also benefit from market influence. On the other hand, they realize they are still winners if there is no adverse impact from the outside market influence. As a matter of fact, if our earnings growth is strong enough, we may actually be a winner with an adverse market impact. If all my stocks have the same P-E ratios in five years as they have today, my appreciation should be directly related to the increase in the earnings of my companies. This is the influence of the company on my stock price, the one I really want.

You might quickly point out that we have to pay more in terms of higher P-E ratios to buy the high-grade growth stocks with strong and consistent earnings records. You would be right, and this is one of the risks that you have to take into account using the growth-stock theory. A helpful exercise I use is to calculate how long it might be before a particular company produces earnings per share that will make my purchase price very reasonable. If I have to pay 20 times earnings for a particular stock, I try to figure out how long it will be before the company doubles its earnings, so that my initial price becomes only 10 times earnings. If the answer is five or six years, my purchase is pretty speculative. The growth stocks that attract me are ones where the period to achieve a conservative initial cost, such as 10 times earnings, seems reasonably short, say two or three years, and the certainty of these higher earnings materializing is rather good. A lovely growth stock, therefore, is a company that you believe has a high certainty of increasing its earnings at an excellent rate, say 20%, and that you are able to buy for a very reasonable price, say 10 times earnings. Do not hesitate to give me your suggestions of any companies you know like this that I should consider.

Whether we mean to or not, each of us involved in this stock selection business builds up certain personal standards in the selection process, which gradually become almost instinctive through constant use. We are looking at growth rates and the probability of the company attaining them, P-E ratios, and other analytical tools, some of which we looked at in table 8.2. After a while, I do not think we change these approaches much; certainly we don't change them as rapidly as the market changes. In my own case, I find that as the market goes up and the stocks I am coveting become more expensive, I have a harder time buying them. Everything seems expensive. When the market has had a strong period, I worry more about the stocks I own getting too expensive. The reverse is true on the downside, because then there seem to be more companies selling at prices that I regard as attractive. I suspect that what is happening is that my analytical approaches and standards are not changing as fast as the market. If I am accustomed to paying 15 times earnings for a 10% growth rate, and the market moves up to a point where it is 20 times earnings for a 10% growth rate, most stocks will seem unattractive to me because my mind has not adjusted to the new world as fast as the market. This intellectual lag can be very helpful over a period of time since it makes stocks seem more expensive when they are high and cheaper, and more attractive when they are low.

We believers in the growth-stock theory occasionally make it sound too easy. The idea is that we simply buy a good growth company, and even if we are wrong in our market timing, the company's earnings will bail us out and make us right. It is worth keeping in mind that the theory is dependent on future earnings, which do not always materialize. When forecasting earnings, we certainly make judgments. Accounting procedures permit management to have quite an influence on even currently reported earnings, so the first question to ask ourselves before we forecast next year's earnings is what the current earnings of the company we are studying really are. Second, we might consider the *quality* of earnings, how sustainable the earnings are from year to year or whether this business is susceptible to many surprises. A third question I ask myself in studying a company has to do with the growth rate. What has the growth rate of earnings been and what is it likely to be? Most fast-growing companies have a tendency to slow down as they grow. The danger in buying growth stocks, therefore, is that we will pay too high a price for a company in which the earnings growth slows down or stops. If I buy what I think is a lovely stock today, and the market starts going to pot tomorrow, I fully expect my lovely stock to wilt with the rest of the garden. This is market influence, so it won't bother me much, since I did not buy it for tomorrow anyway. As the quarterly earnings reports come out, however, and the earnings turn out to be a lot less than I expected, I am in trouble. When our judgment is wrong on a growth stock, the opportunity to lose money abounds.

The third group who do well investing in common stocks is a rather small group of capable analysts who study companies in great detail and buy stocks frequently not well recognized by, or interesting to, most of us investors. These people use the so-called *value approach* to common stock selection, one I wish I had the time and intellect to use more frequently. The approach generally requires a very in-depth analysis of the company by very patient investors who buy their stocks on the basis of price relative to intrinsic values, balance-sheet assets, unrecognized future-earnings capabilities, and other similar values. These holdings can be very frustrating in bull markets, because these stocks are frequently overlooked by the market both ways—they may not go down when the market goes down, but they also have a tendency not to go up when the market goes up. Over a period of time, however, value investors can produce excellent results, partly because their in-depth analysis allows them to buy at attractive prices without as much downside exposure as occurs occasionally with a growth stock.

One small company I keep buying will probably earn a dollar a share this year, generally sells between $6 and $7 a share, and has a $6 book value. Its earnings have increased by 10% to 15% in each of the last five years. Furthermore, the company could be earning $2 a share in another four or five years. I have seen one research report on this company in the last three years. I regard myself as analytical, patient, and a *value* investor. So far, the market regards me as wrong.

Over the years, two approaches to common stock analysis seem to have developed, whether the ultimate aim is a value investment or a growth-stock investment. One approach is called the *top-down approach*; the second is called the *bottoms-up approach*. The top-down approach suggests that we start with what might be called global economics, work down to industries or sectors, and finally down to companies with the idea of selecting the best company in a particular area. The bottoms-up approach suggests that we look deeply at a particular company, get to know that company well enough to acquire conviction on its value, and, therefore, what might happen to its stock. It is a little embarrassing to admit that I am not quite sure which group, if either, I fit. If the top-down approach requires that I forecast the market, I will not be accepted in that group. If the bottoms-up approach requires that I do not try to relate the particular company to its economic environment, that group would not accept me either.

Let me suggest an approach on this selection problem that has been enormously helpful to me for years. Back in the late 1950s, I had the good fortune to spend some time with a fellow from Boston named Horace Nichols (Nick), who has been retired for some time but was absolutely one of the best security analysts I have ever met. At that time, the professional managers of sizable sums were still allocating a certain percentage of their portfolios to various industries—the chemicals, the rails, the steels, etc. What Nick and I concluded, or he did and I adopted, was that the external environment in which a company operated had very important impacts on the results of the company. This external environment, however, was not necessarily a function of an easily categorized industry. What we wanted to look at were companies that were beneficiaries and not victims of very strong and consistent economic trends, trends that cut through the economy well beyond particular industries. If we could identify these trends, we could ask ourselves whether a particular company was a beneficiary or a victim of the pertinent trends influencing its business, and thereby buy companies with a favorable economic environment to produce outstanding results. You could work from the top down or the bottom up. In other words, you could look at a particular company and then ask yourself, What is the economic environment in which this company operates? Is it a beneficiary or a victim? From the top down, you could look first at what trends were strong and consistent in the country. In the 1950s, for example, Americans were working shorter hours with longer vacations and being paid at rates that gave them a much higher degree of discretionary spending. Using the trends approach, Walt Disney looked better than Bethlehem Steel because the economic trends were working well for Disney and against Bethlehem Steel.

Some of the trends beginning in the 1950s have become obvious today. Think about women in the work force (Liz Claiborne), America's health kick (the drug companies), the demographics of the aged (the drug companies, again), the internationalization of our markets (Reuters Holdings, in the financial area). When you think about the impact of external trends on different companies, it becomes obvious that the Penn. Central was a wreck waiting to happen as soon as we built the Pennsylvania Turnpike and our national highway system.

We now live in a world of dinks and oinks and yuppies and aarps and lawyers and cockroaches, and they create the external environments within which our companies operate. One of my favorite clients years ago was an elderly lady who went to Kaufmann's department store, not to buy things—"she didn't need a thing"—but to watch what the other women were buying. Therefore, she bought Revlon in the 1950s, at a time when women were consistently applying pounds of makeup per face per year, instead of U.S. Steel, into which the professional investors were still putting 5% of their portfolios. My message here is that when you read an annual report or research report, or whatever you read about a company that interests you, ask yourself what strong economic trends influence this company and whether this company is a beneficiary or a victim of these trends. You do not have to be a professional securities analyst to ask yourself these questions. As a matter of fact, some of your best security analysis might be done in a grocery or department store.

What I have said above does not preclude the very desirable goal of knowing as much as you possibly can about a company you are thinking of buying, one you own now, or one you are thinking of selling. Understanding your company and reflecting on its economic environment are both worthy exercises in evaluating and forecasting the company's long-term influence on its stock price. If you are involved in your own common stock selection and investing a chunk of your savings, you might think of giving the effort as much time as you take to buy a lawn mower. One of my own rules, which I occasionally break, usually to my regret, is that I should understand the company's products and business very clearly before I buy the stock. In an increasingly technical and scientific world, this little rule is not always as easy to follow as it sounds. I can't expect you to spend as much time as you would in buying a car, but spend a little time thinking about the company. Despite my advice, I will confess that I generally learn more about a company after I have owned it a while than I had learned before I bought it. Fortunately, there is no rule against continuing to learn.

Let me give you one more important reason for knowing as much about your company as you can. Knowledge helps give us conviction, and conviction helps move us away from the psychological norm, otherwise known as the *herd*. If you know your company well and you are pleased with how your company is doing, the fact that the stock market and the price for your stock is currently going down rapidly just does not bother you as much. If your company, and its stock, however, is nothing more to you than a price in the *Wall Street Journal*, you are very likely to join the herd, selling low and buying high.

Textbooks on common stock selection are almost bound to recognize management as a critical ingredient in the success of a company, and certainly we have plenty of books from Peter Drucker and others suggesting successful management approaches. We all know management is important, and we all spend time evaluating them. But, would you rather have a good management in a lousy industry or a lousy management in a good industry? Fortunately, you don't have to answer the question. What we are usually looking for is a good company in a good business with a good management. Friends keep sending me books on this subject with the faint hope they will improve my approach toward evaluating managements. In appreciation I skim the books. My approach toward management is about as subjective as you can get—the most important ingredient being whether I actually like the managers as people. Yes, I want to know whether they are interested in increasing shareholders' value, and how they are going to increase it, but if I really don't like them as people, I probably won't buy their stock anyway. Aside from liking them personally, I am very interested in learning what their fellow employees think of them and whether the people seem to enjoy working at the company. How's that for sophistication?

All of us who have followed the progression of management books over the years have a theory as to how management should run its business. Going back a few decades, management has moved from the *jungle fighter* to the *organization man* to the *gamesman*. All those management texts seem to make sense to me at the time I read them, and then a year or so later we get a new and better theory. So that you can have a little fun about ten years from now, I submit my forecast that the top-flight managements of the 1990s will adopt an approach called *participatory management*. Management will get a lot of direction on how to run the company from the people who work there. More specifically, managements will have enough self-confidence to expose their ideas to people up and down the ladder, and employees, in turn, will have enough confidence in management to express their own ideas to the managers. This will certainly flatten out the organizational chart when the fourth guys down on the current chart will talk to the CEOs and tell them how to run their business. The CEOs, for a change, will have to listen to how they have been screwing up, but they will make better decisions as a product of it.

An uncommon recommendation relative to stock selection is that you engage in a certain amount of self-study. I suspect that it takes some time and experience to know yourself and to have some awareness of your capabilities and/or lack thereof, but the knowledge is certainly worth the effort. For example, I personally seem to enjoy down markets a good bit more than most people. This is helpful to me, because it allows me to buy more stock in a good company if the adverse price activity is simply a result of a short-term market decline and the company I like is doing as well as or better than I expected. Unfortunately, I also have a surfeit of pride that keeps me from recognizing my errors as promptly as I should and curing them accordingly, by selling the stock. Like most people, I have periods of months or years in which I feel I can shoot six in a row from midcourt and have them all swish right through. At other times, I feel I can't make a lay-up. If you are the same, don't get discouraged. One of the questions I ask myself continually as I get older is whether I am adjusting and changing enough or whether I am simply getting more conservative as most people do when they get older. Maybe we *should* become more conservative as we get older. I have taken the oath, however, that I will keep taking risks and keep playing the game as long as I can. Therefore, Hunter kids, I will probably blow your inheritance, so plan accordingly.

If you enjoy the subject of common stock selection, and don't leave it entirely to your investment adviser, let me suggest a few books with which you can spend anywhere from a little to an enormous amount of time:

Graham, Benjamin, and Dodd, David, L. *Security Analysis: Principles and Techniques.* 4th rev. ed. New York: McGraw-Hill, 1988. Benjamin Graham is properly known as the Father of Financial Analysis. The first edition was published in 1934. My copy is the third edition (1951). To the casual student, this book is heavy, so I would suggest you spend a little time with it at the beginning and the end of your self-study course.

Graham, Benjamin. *The Intelligent Investor: A Book of Practical Counsel.* Rev. ed. New York: Harper & Row, 1985. This is Graham's second classic. Much easier reading and a good place to start for the serious student.

Fisher, Philip A. *Common Stocks and Uncommon Profits.* Rev. ed. New York: Harper & Row, 1984. This book originally came out in 1958, at a time when I was trying to put a structure or framework on my own approach toward common stock investing. It had enormous impact on me and my thinking. It is still worth reading today.

Ellis, Charles D. *Investment Policy.* Homewood, Ill.: Dow Jones–Irwin, 1985. This is a short but excellent book on investment policy for an institution or an investor with a very large sum of money. If Ellis had written a similar book for the individual investor, he would have saved me a lot of time.

Lynch, Peter S., with Rothchild, John. *One Up on Wall Street: How to Use What You Already Know to Make Money in the Market.* New York: Simon & Schuster, 1989. The amazing thing about Lynch is that he did so very well with so much money to manage. At first blush, the book seems shallow and glib, but it's deep enough to be read two or three times.

Ellis, Charles D., ed. *Classics, An Investor's Anthology.* Homewood, Ill.: Dow Jones–Irwin, 1989. A collection of writings on investment subjects dating back to 1929, this is my favorite book on the history of investment policy and security selection. For people who really enjoy this subject, it's great. *Classics II* (1991) has now been published, but I have not had time to read it.

Group II — The Cautious Offense

If Group II doesn't ring a bell, go back to table 5.1 (page 54), our balance sheet, and notice that I included the telephone company and a very conservative common stock fund as Group IIs. Group II implies that it is possible to acquire ownership, buy a stock, and yet be reasonably conservative while doing so. The aim of this section of the portfolio is to be quiet, that is, to go down slowly while the rest of the stock market is going down rapidly, and to make a profit. Notice that I put making a profit as the secondary, not the primary, aim. I don't think we should ever buy a stock unless we expect to make a profit; there is simply too much inherent risk in ownership to expose yourself without expecting to make a profit. In Group II stock investing, however, the approach is simply that I want the stocks to behave better in down markets, and this aim is somewhat stronger than the aim of expecting a substantial profit.

What I consider to be Group II stocks are those companies engaged in a very basic business with the demand for their product quite stable and inelastic, a virtual necessity, and little altered by an economic recession (e.g., utilities, telephone companies). Most people equate Group II stocks with high-income production, but, remember, you can have high-income stocks with all the risk of Group IVs, and plenty of them are that risky. Incidentally, years ago common stocks yielded more than bonds, and it was almost unanimously considered proper that they should do so. After all, there was risk in common stocks and not in bonds. The fallacy, of course, was that in the long term stocks could appreciate and bonds would mature. My, how the world has changed: We now get 8% on our bonds and only 3% on our stocks.

When I look at Group II's recent history, I smile at my own naïveté. As recently as the early 1980s, I would have included in Group II most electric utilities, a good number of our telephone companies, quite a few of our best-known food companies, and what I thought to be quiet, conservatively run banks. Certainly, we could have, and still can, included a quiet common stock mutual

fund. These all appealed to me as attractive approaches to ownership for people with conservative investment policies or for people
who were pretty scared by this stock market business or required a
higher level of current income.

Now we can see what occurred with these companies during
the 1980s and how they differed from my expectations. The electric
utilities perhaps were not too surprising. To a certain extent, they
are, by nature, surrogates for fixed income investments and live in a
regulated environment. If anything surprised me about the utilities
over the last 10 or 15 years, it is probably how willing the regula-
tory bodies have been to permit some utilities to become financially unsound. I never would have guessed the number of utilities
that would have some financial difficulty leading to dividend cuts
as we have seen in the last 10 or 15 years. Surprising to me on the
upside were two of the groups—telephone companies and food
companies. The *quiet* telephone companies have produced terrific
earnings and are now regarded more as growth stocks. We *little old
ladies* look pretty smart in retrospect. The food companies that, in
the early 1980s, were selling at seven times earnings and 7% yields
also began to be regarded as growth stocks. Some of the best, like
Nabisco and General Foods, were gobbled up by other companies
at prices that once again made us little old ladies look pretty smart.
The opposite occurred with the *quiet* banks. What we discovered
recently is that there do not seem to be any quiet banks: All the
quiet banks have been making aggressive loans in less-developed
countries like Texas and in real estate developments where people
don't want to live or work. If there is something to be learned from
these surprises, it appears to me that Group IIs, over a period of
time, can move both ways a good bit faster than I expected.

At the moment, it is very difficult to find stocks that I truly
consider Group IIs. I am looking for companies in defensive industries with low betas that sell at reasonable P-E ratios and generate
a decent dividend. Perhaps I should look more at some balanced
(bonds and blue-chip stocks) or conservative common stock mutual
funds as functional equivalents for Group II stocks.

While we are discussing the Group II area, let me throw in another irritating concept, the subject of buying stocks for income. With perhaps a little hyperbole, I take the position that, if you can afford to, you should forget about dividends. If I were to generalize on the investing errors I have made over the years, the largest category by far would be titled Attempts to Get Inordinately Good Current Return. The same generalities that apply to the junk-bond trap could be applied to conservative common stock investing, that is, that the measure of a stock over a period of time should be more related to its total return, appreciation plus dividends. Too many investors pay too much attention to only the current dividend.

Worth considering in this regard is the origin of a dividend. A company produces earnings over the period of a year, and a board of directors presumably makes a decision to retain a certain portion of those earnings and to pay the shareholders a dividend with a portion of those earnings. Now, a rapidly growing company has a great need and use for funds, and will characteristically lead the board to the decision that they should retain the earnings and benefit the shareholders best by reinvesting in the company. If the dividend is a very large percentage of the earnings, the implication is that the board has studied the company and concluded that the company does not have superb uses for the earnings. We cannot ignore the elements of consistency and continuity in dividend policies that strongly impact on the board's decision. Nevertheless, when we leave our retained earnings in the company, they still belong to us shareholders, and when we get them in cash, we pay taxes on them. If you need a useful guide in terms of your own actions, the next time you look at a company and are attracted by the size of its dividend, do a little calculation and figure out how much the incremental return over a normal dividend rate will improve your standard of living. In most cases, the added income will not change your lifestyle.

Find me some good Group IIs. I have a lot of little old lady friends, some of whom are 35-year-old men, and the number of companies I carry in Group II has been shrinking constantly for a decade.

GROUP III — THE BALANCED OFFENSE

Group III is the bulwark of most common stock portfolios. It consists of the type of companies you see listed in the DJIA and in the S&P 500, that is, the blue-chip, well-known companies and the high-grade growth stocks. The aim of the investor with Group III is not to play defense; it is what you might call a balanced offense. The primary aim for most of us, of course, is to do a lot better than the rate of inflation over a period of time. Look at the DJIA chart in table 8.2, because these are blue-chip, mostly Group III, stocks. Look at it and compare it with the inflation rate. It does not include income, like the bond charts. How well high-grade growth stocks have hedged inflation is clearly demonstrated by tables 8.2 and 8.3, so if these relationships did not sink in, go back and spend another ten minutes with the tables. If necessary, read chapter 8 again. Frankly, being human, our aim is usually greater than just beating inflation: We want our good stocks to go up a lot, and we do not want to own the ones that go down a lot.

Most of the general common stock concepts I have expressed apply very strongly to Group III selections. You can use the growth-stock theory or the value-stock approach and you can go top-down or bottoms-up. Since Group III includes most of the better-known corporations in the United States from Abbott Labs to Xerox, it is a very large group, and for most of us it is helpful to categorize or classify these companies. For example, you may have a tendency toward high-grade growth stocks or cyclical heavy-industry stocks. Peter Lynch, in *One Up on Wall Street*, does a good job at segmenting Group IIIs when he talks about "stalwarts" and "fast growers" and "turnarounds" and "slow growers." Some analysts are better at certain areas than others. I have never done very well at "cyclicals" or "turnarounds," so I try to avoid them. Occasionally, though, I take the plunge. To borrow one of Warren Buffett's analogies, I have a "toad" in my portfolio that I have "kissed" for three years without it showing any signs of ever becoming a princess. The stock is analytically fascinating, but it still remains a toad. More recently, Buffett gave us some further wise advice relative to our own capabilities when he made the comment that he had done better avoiding "dragons" than slaying them.

One theory espoused by some analysts is the so-called *efficient-market theory*, which contends that all the public information available on a company is reflected in the current stock price. Therefore, the market price each day is the appropriate price for the stock and only new information on the company should alter relative price action. I presume from this that you could just decide from the betas how much risk you want to take to build your portfolio and end your analysis.

A second intellectual approach is the so-called *random-walk theory*, which implies we will all come out the same in our stock selection over an extended period of time.

I do not subscribe to either of these theories, especially for individual investors. I advocate that we do a great deal of homework on individual companies, their financial measurements and prospects, and virtually no work on forecasting the general direction of the stock market. I agree that the market for major companies, reflecting the enormous amount of research work that is done today, is more *efficient* than it was years ago. To shed some light on the subject, I included table 14.1, which shows the monetary change in the 30 Dow Industrials from the beginning of 1981 through the end of 1990. Take a moment to look at it.

It should be obvious, even to the random-walkers, that it sure mattered *which* stocks you owned, given the wide difference in performance. Still, this was a remarkably prosperous time for the stock market generally, so for balance, and your reading pleasure, I added table 14.2, which shows the prices for the 30 Dow Industrials in the ten years ending December 31, 1974. This shows that you can hold a lot of well-known companies for ten years and not make any money (27 out of 30 during this decade), but it still mattered plenty which ones you owned. I had so much fun looking at these charts that I included table 14.3, which shows the ten years from 1974 through 1983. I suspect you can use these tables to conclude anything you would like about Group III investing, but I

Table 14.1

Dow Jones Industrial Stocks

The results in market value of $10,000 invested for ten years in each of 30 Dow Jones Industrial Stocks on January 1, 1981, exclusive of dividend income. The total investment in the 30 stocks was $300,000.

	Market Value 12/31/90
Philip Morris	$ 95,727
Coca-Cola	83,596
Merck	63,628
McDonald's	60,491
Procter & Gamble	50,309
Woolworth	48,889
Westinghouse Electric	38,482
General Electric	37,469
Boeing	34,706
AT&T	33,611
Minnesota Mining & Manufacturing	29,068
Du Pont	26,250
Exxon	25,674
International Paper	25,476
American Express	20,497
Alcoa	19,329
IBM	16,648
Sears, Roebuck	16,639
United Technologies	15,697
General Motors	15,278
Primerica	15,062
Chevron	14,598
Eastman Kodak	13,427
Texaco	12,604
USX	12,323
Goodyear	11,797
Union Carbide	9,776
Allied Signal	7,470
Bethlehem Steel	5,592
Navistar	878
Total	**$861,091**

Table 14.2

Dow Jones Industrial Stocks

The results in market value of $10,000 invested for ten years in each of 30 Dow Jones Industrial Stocks on January 1, 1965, exclusive of dividend income. The total investment in the 30 stocks was $300,000.

	Market Value 12/31/74
Procter & Gamble	$ 20,000
Eastman Kodak	18,159
International Paper	10,916
Esmark	9,654
American Brands	9,133
United Aircraft	7,471
Sears, Roebuck	7,466
U. S. Steel	7,451
Johns-Manville	7,290
Alcoa	7,287
Exxon	7,171
General Electric	7,158
Bethlehem Steel	7,083
American Can Company	6,744
Standard Oil of California	6,686
AT&T	6,538
Union Carbide	6,516
Owens-Illinois	6,459
International Nickel	6,399
Allied Chemical	5,833
Goodyear	5,692
International Harvester	5,223
Anaconda	5,168
Texaco	4,765
Westinghouse Electric	4,706
General Foods	4,434
Du Pont	3,830
Woolworth	3,394
General Motors	3,142
Chrysler	1,189
Total	**$212,957**

Table 14.3

Dow Jones Industrial Stocks

The results in market value of $10,000 invested for ten years in each of 30 Dow Jones Industrial Stocks on January 1, 1974, exclusive of dividend income. The total investment in the 30 stocks was $300,000.

	Market Value 12/31/83
United Technologies	$ 61,053
American Brands	36,744
Owens-Illinois	24,211
General Foods	21,632
Westinghouse Electric	21,576
Goodyear	19,918
Standard Oil of California	19,786
IBM	19,776
Woolworth	19,116
General Electric	18,611
American Can Company	18,564
Alcoa	18,505
Union Carbide	18,388
General Motors	16,125
Exxon	15,883
Procter & Gamble	12,364
AT&T	12,269
Texaco	12,213
U. S. Steel	12,110
Allied Corporation	11,378
International Paper	11,346
Merck	11,192
Minnesota Mining & Manufacturing	10,577
Du Pont	9,811
Sears, Roebuck	9,252
Bethlehem Steel	8,636
Manville Corporation	6,667
Eastman Kodak	6,563
International Harvester	4,466
Inco	4,149
Total	**$492,881**

Table 14.4

Dow Jones Industrial Stocks

The results in market value of $10,000 invested for ten years in each of 30 Dow Jones Industrial Stocks on January 1, 1990, exclusive of dividend income. The total investment in the 30 stocks was $300,000.

	Market Value 12/31/99
American Express	$ 162,068
International Harvester [1]	113,939
General Electric	92,734
Primerica [2]	85,609
Procter & Gamble	62,163
Coca-Cola	59,744
E. I. Du Pont de Nemours & Co.	55,108
Merck	51,277
United Technologies	46,847
McDonald's Corp.	46,237
International Business Machines	44,031
Aluminum Co. of America	43,901
Exxon [3]	32,225
Union Carbide	27,385
Minnesota Mining & Manufacturing	25,314
Chevron	25,063
AT&T	23,901
General Motors	20,668
Boeing	20,212
Sears, Roebuck	19,804
International Paper	19,716
Eastman Kodak	19,315
Texaco	18,372
Westinghouse Electric [4]	16,937
Allied-Signal [5]	16,307
Philip Morris	16,142
Goodyear Tire & Rubber	12,369
U. S. Steel [6]	8,691
Bethlehem Steel	4,467
F. W. Woolworth [7]	2,121
Total	**$1,192,668**

[1] Finished period as Navistar International Corp.
[2] Finished period as Citigroup Inc.
[3] Finished period as Exxon Mobil Corp.
[4] Finished period as CBS Corp.
[5] Finished period as Honeywell International Inc.
[6] Includes the value of Marathon Oil Co. shares added during the period.
[7] Finished period as Venator Group, Inc.

will simply say that it makes a lot of difference what you own for a decade. Interestingly, only two companies, General Electric and Exxon, appeared in the top half of the 30 Dow stocks in each of the three decades.

I play a little game every time I see charts like these. I draw a line between the top 15 and the bottom 15 and see how many of the top 15 I have in client portfolios versus the bottom 15. Then I try to figure out why. Personally, I have discovered only two broad techniques that I believe will keep most of my selections in the top 15 stocks over a decade. I mentioned both previously, but they bear repeating: (1) Try to learn as much as you can about the company; and (2) think about it in its broader context, the external environment, and whether it is working for or against the company.

One of the nice things I discovered about Wall Street research is that it is generally free to an individual. An analyst works very hard on a research report, manages to talk a few people in his own firm into reading it, but is absolutely delighted when someone like myself actually wants to read a copy. In the securities business, it is a lot better to be able to recognize good work than actually be able to do it. It is also a lot easier. If someone asked me how many times I think I have been the first person to have a very creative and successful stock selection idea, my answer would be once. The stock increased six times over a two- or three-year period. The crazy thing is I picked the wrong one of the two stocks I was considering at the time; the other one did better longer. Every other good idea I have ever had was borrowed from somebody else.

GROUP IV — THE AGGRESSIVE OFFENSE

Before I say anything about my favorite investment area, Group IV, let me repeat very clearly that you do not absolutely require Group IV common stocks to balance a portfolio, fight inflation, or produce reasonable rates of return over a period of years. A good portfolio does not necessarily have to go below Group III.

The aim of Group IV stocks is very simple—to make a large amount of money! Almost all the investments I make in Group IV stocks are in smaller companies that I want to see grow rapidly and have their stock prices at least track their growth rates. Since I suggested that your division of assets be on the basis of quality or safety of principal, I also include in Group IV sizable companies that are *turnarounds* and speculative enough so that they simply do not qualify to be Group IIIs.

The approach toward selecting Group IVs differs little from buying a high-grade growth stock or a good value stock except that it is easier. Smaller companies with narrower product lines are a lot more easily understood than most of our major industrial concerns. As a matter of fact, that is one thing I am looking for in Group IV, a company that is a leader in a particular niche or narrow industry, with distinctive products and perhaps new products that will allow them to grow faster than most larger businesses.

Because the smaller companies are less well researched and frequently *underowned* by institutions, you are more likely to find a lower P-E ratio compared to the growth rate. Be aware that the reverse can also be true: P-E ratios of Group IVs are occasionally very high, far beyond those that pertain to the blue-chip, growth-stock area. Certainly, Group IVs lend themselves to the question I mentioned previously: How long will it be before the price I pay now is reasonable? If I have to pay 20 times earnings for that pretty little company that is currently growing at 20% a year, it will be 3.6 years before my cost basis becomes 10 times earnings. That can well be long enough, since the earnings just might not grow 20% annually.

Incidentally, if a company or its stock seems pretty risky to you but you still find it very attractive, simply make a smaller-than-normal investment in the company. As I mentioned previously, there is nothing wrong with building a concept like half-normal into your investment policy.

Group IVs are also a great area for finding *value* investments as well as growth stocks. The research reports may be few in number. If you read the writings of the great security analysts over the last 20 or 30 years (starting with Benjamin Graham, of course), you might believe that what good analysts are all looking for is a great company, the *supercompany*. The idea is to buy a stock and have the company perform beautifully almost year after year. Recognizing companies like this early in their growth periods is certainly not easy, but it is a worthy quest. The analytical trade-off, of course, is the fact that we make more errors in buying smaller, rapidly growing companies. Group IV errors can be pretty expensive. They are not all supercompanies.

As you consider Group IV stocks and your own investment policy, it might be helpful for you to divide the group into large companies and small companies. The larger companies that I include in Group IV have a speculative aspect to them, a quality deficiency, which provides too much risk to include the stocks in Group III. A typical example is a large company that hits very adverse circumstances and becomes speculative enough to drop from Group II or III to Group IV. Many of these companies are then characterized as speculative turnaround situations.

My comment that Group IV investments are not necessary to achieve very satisfactory investment results in no way should discourage conservative investors from buying Group IV stocks once they have the financial stability to do so. Some years ago, I attended the annual meeting of a small software company, a meeting mostly attended by young analytical types who I am sure understood more about the products of this company than I. The stock had performed very well, and it was a real pleasure to see two of my little-old-lady clients (who *were* literally little old ladies) sitting in the back row of the meeting with big smiles on their faces.

Group V — The Long Bomb

What is a Group V stock? Well, I define a Group V stock, and also Groups VI, VII, and VIII, as common stocks in which there is so much risk that they really do not make good investment sense. A lottery ticket might be a good Group VIII. Do people occasionally make money from these types of investments? Absolutely.

Somebody wins lotteries, but more money flows into lotteries than flows out to investors. Certainly, a few of these companies start out as very speculative and gradually work their way to become enormously successful enterprises over a period of years. The point is that many investment possibilities are more likely to be poor investments than good investments, and the odds are therefore against the individual investor. I admit, however, that a capable securities analyst can occasionally look at what many of us consider to be a Group V or VI and recognize it as an attractive Group IV because of a unique knowledge of the company or the business. I frequently think of a case where a venture capitalist invested some years ago in a genetic engineering company and eventually made a sale of such size that his gain was noted in the newspapers. This was more than luck, but I also admit that had I been offered the stock at the outset, there is no way I would have bought it. Therefore, having outstanding analytical capabilities and judgment can allow certain investors to assume more intelligent and greater risk than others.

Keep in mind, too, that companies can move both ways in your portfolio. I have a couple of Group Vs that started as Group IVs and worked their way down through poor performance. Most people who engage in Group V common stock investing are simply interested in *making a killing*, buying low-priced stocks or following unfounded rumors or tips. If you find yourself intrigued or tempted by very speculative investments, promise you will do one exercise. Find the total number of shares outstanding and multiply that times the price of the stock to determine the total market value of the company. Now, compare that figure with this year's, last year's, or even next year's sales and earnings to see how expensive this company really is.

If, by chance, you have kissed quite a few "toads" and none of them has turned into a princess (or prince), one possible conclusion is that you are not much good at kissing toads. Remember, to be successful there is no requirement that you kiss any toads, and certainly there is no rule that says you have to kiss all the toads.

After all this discussion on buying a stock, you might well ask the question of when should you sell a stock. I will suggest a few guidelines. Some successful investors employ set rules for guiding both their buying and selling of individual stocks. Illustration: "If it goes down 15% after you bought it, sell it." Personally, I am not much for firm rules on selling. As a matter of fact, some of the old Wall Street expressions, such as "no tree grows to the sky" or "water seeks its own level," may be mildly humorous, but they are not much in the way of guidance. Certainly, if our policy dictates it, we have to sell something; so the question is, Which of my stocks do I sell? An easy answer with a fair amount of validity is to sell your losers. Swallow your pride, do not wait for it to get back where it started, sell it. When we buy a stock, we normally have expectations for the company to do certain wonderful things for us, such as produce good earnings. When these wonderful things do not happen, their absence raises a red flag. When our analysis is wrong, we should think about selling the stock. Do not think about selling the stock if the company is doing fine and the market simply declines. In good markets we occasionally get lucky and our errors are concealed by the ebullience of the market. Our stock has appreciated, but think about selling it anyway. Certainly, our capital gains tax is an incentive to eliminate our clunkers. The one period during the year when my clients are happy with my errors is when they are doing their income taxes. It is interesting that we refer to our errors as *tax losses*. You do not hear many people talk about *tax gains*. In any event, an important control is to keep one stock from ruining your performance. Sell your errors before they get serious.

Over a period of time, try to understand your own psychological makeup and adjust for it in both buying and selling. Personally, I wish I were better at selling. Prices for good stocks seem to go a lot higher than I think they should, so my own problem with selling is not getting rid of the clunkers but selling too soon on the upside. Strangely enough, I think as I get older my time horizon or my patience seems to get longer rather than shorter. Therefore, I tell myself that I am getting better at selling because I do less of it than I used to. I try to remember what Philip Fisher said when he would sell a very successful company: "Almost never."

If this business of investing well is a function of having a good, consistent investment policy and selecting good common stocks, I certainly picked the easier of the two subjects by concentrating on investment policy. What we can learn about individual security selection is endless, and I recognize that I only scratched the surface in this chapter. As Christy Mathewson, the great pitcher, said, "I'd rather be lucky than good," but he practiced a lot. As the story goes, when he was a kid, he cut a hole in the barn door and threw baseballs at it by the hour. For most people, the task of selecting individual stocks is best left to the professional. What you can do, however, is to make sure you know where your securities fit into your investment policy, and certainly each of us can develop a sensitivity to economic trends—at least we can know what is going on in the supermarkets and malls of America.

.

Common Stocks in 2001— Where We Keep Learning…

I can remember when the first batch of the original book was delivered to my office. I had a terrible reaction: "Everything I know is in that book, and if it didn't have thick covers, it would be a pamphlet." If it weren't for chapter 14, "Common Stock Investing," it would be a pamphlet even with the thick covers.

Please remember, kids, this book is about investment policy, making important decisions you will follow in your investing process. This chapter is intended to address the many policy questions that relate to common stocks and hopefully give you a useful approach. It is not intended to tell you explicitly how to pick a stock, although picking stocks is to some of us (me) a real fun part of the business. I'll be pleased if I give you concepts or approaches that will allow you to question the stocks you're holding or considering.

In this addendum to chapter 14, my comments are amendments and in some cases reiterations on specific points made in the original chapter. Even I was surprised at how little I'd learned:

GENERAL STOCK COMMENTS

Risk

"The primary goal of common stock investing is to play offense, to make money." With the stock market at such historically high levels, this comment is even truer today than it was ten years ago. Generally speaking, there is too much risk in buying a stock today to do so for any reason other than to produce a profit. This is not the same as saying we should maximize our risk in each selection for the maximum gain. I'm simply saying that there's a lot more risk in today's world at today's prices than we previously incurred, and more than most investors today realize.

Market Forecasting

At year-end 1995, I had the joy of lunching with three wonderful friends, each of whom had managed a major securities firm for some years. The first subject was not whether the market was going to drop, but what event was going to precipitate the drop. It was a rare event since I couldn't even insert a comment for 20 minutes while they traded brilliance on the forthcoming decline. We're now four years later and the market has experienced its greatest rise in history.

I can also laugh at myself on market forecasting. For years the Economics Club of Pittsburgh has allowed me to join two prominent economists in an annual January "Forecast" luncheon. In 1990 I made the comment that it was a reasonably sure bet that the stock market in the 1990s would most certainly not be as good as the market of the 1980s. We now have seen the 1980s market dwarfed by the explosion of the 1990s. Apparently I can't even forecast the stock market by the decade. Interestingly enough, the number of people who make a living by forecasting the stock market has declined substantially over the last two or three decades.

Join me in repeating the oath and conviction that we cannot forecast the short-term stock market. Our long-term bull market makes it tempting. Resist the temptation. Your conviction that you cannot do so will serve you well.

Having the discipline to stick to your investment policy will make the fluctuations in the market easier to tolerate. Your asset allocation will tell you whether you are in a buying or a selling or a "do nothing" mode.

If the equity portion of your portfolio declines with a market decline, this tells you to buy that good-looking company you had your eye on when it was more expensive.

Stock Picking

Are you going to do your own securities selection, or are you selecting someone else to do it? This is a policy question. Over the years I've come to recognize enormous differences in the abilities of individuals, even professionals, to select stocks that perform well. Each of us can learn a great deal and improve our selection process, but the basic abilities and psychological makeup of each of us somehow translate into wide and apparently permanent variances in security selection ability. Nobody could really teach Ted Williams how to hit. The one thing we can learn from a potential adviser is the process by which he or his firm selects stocks. This person must recognize your needs as an individual and not simply sell you a "product." The most popular products in the securities industry are usually next year's bombs.

Shaving in the Morning

I've found that the impact of your asset allocation policy on the equity portion of your portfolio is just as important in selling stocks as it is in buying them. Approximately 80% of the sales transactions I initiate for clients are precipitated not by a conviction that a particular stock will decline, but by the balance and asset allocation in their portfolios. Fortunately, my decision after reviewing a portfolio is to cut back or shave a certain stock that has performed beautifully and simply has too much influence on the portfolio. We'll reduce it a bit. The portfolio, therefore, is really dictating the cutback in an inordinately large position. I try to shave slowly since I have forever underestimated how high up a stock can go. Shaving is seldom popular with my clients who have learned to love that stock. Certainly I will occasionally eliminate a particular stock entirely, most frequently when I've decided I was wrong in my judgment of the company's performance in the first place. The sooner I recognize this, the better off I'll be. Only occasionally do I eliminate a stock entirely simply because in my view the price has become too high.

The Company versus the Market
I've mentioned the two influences on the price of a stock: the results of the company, and the direction and impact of the market. Different stocks have different degrees of each kind of impact under all market scenarios. In the high stock market, the more appealing stocks to me are those that have a larger company influence and a smaller market influence (frequently an unpopular stock). Even in a very high market there are generally a substantial number of good companies selling at cheap prices. Look over your own securities and see if you can get a feel for how much market exposure you have in each stock versus the influence of the company's operating results. This is something of a seldom employed but useful approach toward measuring your own degree of risk.

Diversification
The number of stocks you hold in your portfolio is a policy decision. Needless to say, if you own 6 stocks, you can expect to have more pronounced ups and downs than if you own 60. If I weren't so old, I would own fewer stocks than I have, but it's very hard to get rid of old favorites with high capital gains tax consequences. For this reason we seem to broaden our portfolios as we broaden our posteriors over the years. One of the problems for mutual fund

investors who own positions in more than one or two funds is that the wonderful results of a particular company just don't matter.

Popular Delusions

At any point in time the market research world is full of concepts and approaches that are momentarily popular and to a certain degree useful. In my hoary old age, however, I find myself somewhat cynical about many of these concepts as guides to good investing. It seems there's a germ of truth in each, or they at least provide buzzwords for definitions of ideas. Otherwise they are generally not very useful in my everyday work. A few examples:

1. *Day trading.* It took me less than a day to reject this idea. Day trading eliminates the positive effects of your company's good work over time and bases your entire investment on vagaries of the unpredictable day-to-day market. I would rather eliminate the market vagaries and depend on my company.

2. *Sector analysis* is used by people who feel they can figure out what particular group of stocks is next going to do well in the market. To me this is much like market forecasting brought down to a specific level. Certainly groups of stocks move together at times, and being aware of these moves can be advantageous. If the drug stocks are having a tough market period because the government is leaning on them heavily, I am more attracted to good drug companies at lower prices and may select one or two, but I don't do so because I think it's the next sector to move. Perhaps I simply don't have enough expertise to endorse sector analysis. I am aware, however, of industry concentrations in a particular portfolio.

3. I even get a little confused on the concepts of *"value"* versus *"growth" investing.* Certainly I endorse the growth-stock theory, but I am also properly accused of buying a lot of value stocks. My response is that I'm using the growth-stock theory by buying a value stock that I fervently hope will grow. If it turns out

that the market subsequently regards my "value" stock as a "growth" stock, I'm probably a real winner because the earnings will go up as I had hoped and the price-earnings ratio will probably go up as I had not necessarily expected. I don't seem to spend much time with value stocks that I don't expect to grow. There, kids, see if you can figure out what I said.

4. I really don't know much about *options* or *other derivatives*, either. I did buy my 95-year-old mother-in-law a "PUT LEAP" on one of her blue-chip stocks we felt was both overvalued with a big capital gain and overconcentrated in her portfolio. I am pleased to say that my mother-in-law outlived the LEAP but made a small bundle when she sold it.

5. *Foreign investing.* A few years ago one of my best friends, who had the chore of selecting money managers for a large sum, said to me at a cocktail party, "Hunter, you absolutely have to get 30% of your assets overseas." Stubborn as I am, that was almost enough to keep me totally domestic. For one thing, accounting differences make it difficult to compare foreign securities with American securities. Furthermore, as debauched as our culture is and our government is, I have more confidence in them than in their foreign counterparts. Occasionally I buy a foreign security, but 10% would be a high figure for me.

"You Have To"

Maybe the important message here is that you don't *have to* take any particular action to invest well. You don't *have to* have so much in small-cap, mid-cap, or large-cap stocks. You don't even *have to* set target prices for the stocks you own. Ten or 15 years ago many people would tell you that you had to use technical analysis before you actually bought a stock. Today we use very little technical analysis. As a matter of fact, you don't even *have to* know very much to be a successful investor. You'll probably be better off if you do only what you or your adviser knows, and don't try to do what you don't know. The most successful investors I know have rather simple portfolios.

Earnings

Ten years ago I spent considerable time discussing earnings, and I'm glad I did, because if anything, the impact of earnings on stock prices has magnified almost to absurdity. Today a stock can lose 30% of its value if the company misses the earnings estimate by a penny. We long-term investors are really trying to gauge future earnings. My old friend Arthur Levitt must have this in mind as he encourages the Securities and Exchange Commission to work with accountants and accounting standards. I try to spend a little time with quarterly and annual reports of my companies because they almost always contain some real clues on what the company might be doing a year from now.

Trends

Probably no concept has provided me with more investing happiness and less investing grief than that of putting a company into the framework of its external economic trends. One of the nice things about this approach is that virtually any of us can use it. A couple of years ago I gave a talk to a captive audience on the trends I saw impacting our small investment firm. This, of course, was an attempt to apply my trends theory to a specific company (our own) in a specific industry, but that's exactly what I would suggest you try to do. You can do it with any company in any specific industry.

To incite you to do more and better work than I, I have included table 14.5, which sets forth a few of the trends I mentioned affecting our firm. You might take a company in which you are interested and make a list of the trends affecting it. Do negatives as well as positives. Yes, I would rather have a great management in a lousy industry than the reverse, but let's try for the best of both.

Psychology

Throughout the book I've touched on certain ethereal subjects like self-analysis with the thought that some self-study can reduce, if not eliminate, some of our personal attributes inhibiting our investment performance. Patience, for example, is a wonderful attribute in investing. Personally I don't have much patience, but I certainly

Table 14.5

Trends Affecting an Investment Firm

Megatrends

1. The rise of the private enterprise system and the decline of the collectivist societies
2. The financial industry's ability to become global very easily and quickly
3. Technological progress and the rapid dissemination of information
4. The increase in people with advanced education
5. The enormous economic success of the United States
6. The understanding and endorsement of the concept of ownership versus lending

National Trends

1. Demographics; the baby boomers moving from tangible to intangible investments
2. Demographics; the growth in the number and percentage of older people who have financial assets
3. The increased number of people of all ages with savings; the affluent society
4. The increased awareness of inflation as an investment consideration
5. The growth in the number of small businesses and people employed by small businesses
6. The advent of the IRA and the nation's awareness of tax considerations in investments
7. The gradual awareness of labor and management of their common interests in a competitive world
8. Greater interest in educating children and planning for retirement
9. Increased number of women in the workplace and two-income families

Industry Trends

1. The growth awareness of alternative investment approaches
2. The enormous growth of mutual funds
3. Technology again; the decline in the cost of executing transactions
4. The availability of outside services to control costs
5. The increase in the number of corporate prospects for investment banking firms
6. Technology again and again; providing immediate information into all areas of the business

Specific Competitive Trends

1. The ready availability of excellent research to all those who seek it
2. An increasing recognition of a focus on clients and asset allocation
3. The gradual elimination of conflicts of interest between brokers and clients
4. An increased ability on the part of the client to evaluate services and capabilities
5. Changes in analytical approach; less market forecasting, more in-depth company research, less technical analysis, more varied alternatives
6. Widely divergent strategic approaches of different firms

You might want to make a list of the positive and negative trends affecting a company that interests you.

have a surfeit of stubbornness, which can work a lot like patience. In my case, the stubbornness is combined with a surfeit of pride; it bugs me when I am wrong, so I have to work at admitting I'm wrong.

I also know I am a little different, since most of America experiences the full joy of greed in the kind of bull market we've had for several years and very little of the misery of fear. As stock prices go up, unlike other things we buy, most people like them better and want to buy more. Somewhat fortunately, as stock prices go up I feel a little more fear than greed. A weirdo like me can't understand why most people like stocks *more* as stock prices go up. Everything else people buy, they like better when the price goes down. Considering our own mental makeup, our strengths and weaknesses, our tolerance for loss, helps us individualize our policy.

GROUP II — THE CAUTIOUS OFFENSE

If by 1990 the appreciation of most of the Group II stocks had pushed them down into Group III, you can be assured that the bull market of the 1990s has pushed virtually all of the remaining Group IIs down into Group III. A great debate today would be whether many of our high-grade Group III stocks have become risky enough through price appreciation and high price-earning ratios to become Group IV stocks. I find myself going into the new century with no names on my list of attractive Group IIs. You were supposed to give me some good ideas.

Incidentally, ten years ago we were experiencing a decrease in the importance of the dividend to the conservative investor in the stock selection process. This trend has continued, partly as a product of the increased volatility in the stock market. This is one security analysis trend I endorse, not giving much weight to the dividend. Picking a loser in Group II remains a much greater sin to me than picking a loser in Group IV. In Group II we are supposed to be investing conservatively and protecting ourselves against disasters. In Group II we are not investing with the idea of substantial fluctuation. In Group IV we expect to bomb occasionally and are not amazed when a bomb goes off.

GROUP III — THE BALANCED OFFENSE

History and usage, even today, make the Dow Jones Average the most popular common indicator of changes in the market. As time goes on, the Standard & Poors 500 Index becomes more popular because of its breadth. Needless to say, the 1990s have been wonderful for both indexes, and the challenge to many investment managers has been keeping up with the DJIA or keeping up with the S&P. Most institutional managers, other than those in the high-tech area, have failed to do so. For a bit of a smile, however, I have added table 14.6 to show the changes in the composition of the DJIA over the last 35 years. As you'll notice, only 19 of the stocks in the current DJIA were in the index at the beginning of 1990, and only 10 of the current stocks were in the index at the beginning of 1965. Certainly the 30 stocks of 1965 didn't keep up with the DJIA over subsequent decades.

My personal interpretation of the older DJIA is that they were pretty good stocks for their decade, but the more modern DJIA presents a case for updating your portfolio occasionally. With a bit of homework I think you could have eliminated most of the same companies that the DJIA has eliminated and done considerably better as a product of your work, even if you reviewed your portfolio once a decade.

The original intent of the indexes was to measure the change in the market. Do they still really do that, or have their sponsors yielded to their competitive instincts?

GROUP IV — THE AGGRESSIVE OFFENSE

Three or four of the current DJIA stocks I would have considered risky enough to be Group IVs ten years ago. I wish I had been smart enough to buy them all then.

There is no shortage of Group IV stocks. Our national prosperity has given us thousands of Group IVs, enough to investigate and evaluate for the next decade. Frankly, I find the process of selection no different from what it was a decade ago, but I am certainly enormously grateful for the information and technological revolution that allows us to collect more material more quickly on a company we want to consider. I am not sure the information we receive today is any better than it used to be, but I suspect it is. Even so, I still make most of my errors in the attractive hunting ground of Group IVs.

GROUP V— THE LONG BOMB

I'm not much for bombs of any kind, but certainly the technological revolution and market explosion this past decade have provided us with an enormous number of available Group V investments, stocks that don't pass analytical muster. You can tell that I am not wild about these opportunities. Perhaps they're characterized by a substantial number of dot coms, where a true financial analysis is virtually impossible for most of us. It's hard enough for me to do Microsoft, Intel, and Cisco. When people ask me about the dot coms, I facetiously say that they're very interesting but my parents insisted I go to school too long for me to buy any of them. I am a very lucky person, but I do not think I am lucky enough to pick successful survivors from the dot coms.

Table 14.6
The Changing Dow

DJIA 01/01/1965	DJIA 01/01/1990	DJIA 01/01/2000
1. Aluminum Co. of America	1. Aluminum Co. of America	1. Alcoa
2. American Telephone & Telegraph Co.	2. American Telephone & Telegraph Co.	2. AT&T Corp.
3. Bethlehem Steel Corp.	3. Bethlehem Steel Corp.	3. E. I. Du Pont de Nemours & Co.
4. E. I. Du Pont de Nemours & Co.	4. E. I. Du Pont de Nemours & Co.	4. Eastman Kodak Co.
5. Eastman Kodak Co.	5. Eastman Kodak Co.	5. Exxon Mobil Corp.*
6. F. W. Woolworth Co.	6. Exxon Corp.*	6. General Electric Co.
7. General Electric Co.	7. F. W. Woolworth Co.	7. General Motors Co.
8. General Motors Co.	8. General Electric Co.	8. International Paper Co.
9. Goodyear Tire & Rubber Co.	9. General Motors Co.	9. Procter & Gamble Co.
10. International Harvester Co.	10. Goodyear Tire & Rubber Co.	10. United Technologies Corp.**
11. International Paper Co.	11. International Harvester Co.	*American Express Co.*
12. Procter & Gamble Co.	12. International Paper Co.	*Boeing Co.*
13. Sears, Roebuck & Co.	13. Procter & Gamble Co.	*Coca-Cola Co.*
14. Standard Oil Co. (New Jersey)	14. Sears, Roebuck & Co.	*Honeywell International Inc.***
15. Texaco Inc.	15. Texaco Inc.	*International Business Machines Corp.*
16. U. S. Steel Corp.	16. U. S. Steel Corp.	*McDonald's Corp.*
17. Union Carbide Corp.	17. Union Carbide Corp.	*Merck & Co.*
18. United Aircraft	18. United Technologies Corp.**	*Minnesota Mining & Manufacturing Co.*
19. Westinghouse Electric Corp.	19. Westinghouse Electric Corp.	*Phillip Morris Cos.*
20. General Foods Co.	*Allied-Signal Inc.*	*Caterpillar Inc.*
21. Allied Chemical	*American Express Co.*	*Citigroup*
22. American Can Co.	*Boeing Co.*	*Hewlett-Packard Co.*
23. American Tobacco	*Chevron Corp.*	*Home Depot Inc.*
24. Anaconda Copper Mining Co.	*Coca-Cola Co.*	*Intel Corp.*
25. Chrysler Corp.	*International Business Machines Corp.*	*J. P. Morgan & Co.*
26. International Nickel Co.	*McDonald's Corp.*	*Johnson & Johnson*
27. Johns-Manville Corp.	*Merck & Co.*	*Microsoft & Co.*
28. Owens-Illinois Glass Co.	*Minnesota Mining & Manufacturing Co.*	*SBC Communications*
29. Standard Oil Co. of California	*Philip Morris Cos.*	*Wal-Mart Stores Inc.*
30. Swift & Co.	*Primerica Corp.*	*Walt Disney Co.*
869.78	**2810.15**	**11357.51**

*Formerly Standard Oil Co. (New Jersey)   **Formerly United Aircraft   ***Formerly Allied-Signal Inc.

CHAPTER 15

Myths and Fears

IT IS FASHIONABLE IN BOOKS OF THIS TYPE TO HAVE A CHAPTER titled "Things You Should Not Do" or "Mistakes Investors Make." Even Philip Fisher in his classic, *Common Stocks and Uncommon Profits*, had a chapter titled "Five Don'ts for Investors" followed by another one titled "Five More Don'ts for Investors." At least once a year I see a don't-do list in some publication. I cannot remember ever reading one with which I had a major disagreement. Therefore, the next time you see one, I suggest you spend a few minutes with it.

Instead of writing a list of things you should not do, however, I would rather address some of the prevalent investing myths and fears that seem to bother a large number of individuals and try to give you some comfort about the very pervasive fear that you do not know very much about this investing business.

It used to bother me years ago that I did not know very much, so I read a lot and studied different approaches to the stock market and investing—but I was still bothered. My first comfort came after a few years when I realized that most everybody else involved in this investing business did not know very much either. This is an endless and vast subject. The second comfort came with the realization that if I knew a good bit about a few things, it was better than knowing a little bit about a lot of things, and that knowing a good bit about a few things was enough to get by.

One of the most prominent fears centers around the idea that *they*, the institutions and professional money managers with unique knowledge or information, make all the money and the individual investor is, therefore, at a great disadvantage. About all you have to do to dismiss this myth is take a look at the lackluster performance of most institutional investors over a period of years. Frankly, I do not expect the major institutions to perform outstandingly well simply because they have so much money to invest that they are almost precluded from being creative in stock selection. Peter Lynch at Fidelity was an aberration by performing well with ever-increasing sums of money. My perception is that many long-term clients of most institutions are reasonably happy by now if their institution keeps up with the market averages. Most do not. To me, the most surprising aspect of institutional managers is how frequently they turn over their portfolios. If they were individual investors, they could be accused of churning their own accounts. As a matter of fact, if my clients turned over their portfolios as frequently as the average institutional investor, I would be the wealthiest guy in the Pittsburgh jail.

A second area of concern about institutions involves their use of momentarily popular strategies with which the layman has no affinity or understanding. This creates in the individual investor a fair degree of fear of the unknown. When you think, however, of the motives behind some of the popular strategies employed by large institutional investors, they appear to be designed more to prohibit terrible performance than to promote good performance. For example, we employ *hedging* when we are not sure what we are doing; we use *indexing* when we want to come out about the same as others; we buy *portfolio insurance* so we won't get clobbered. It seems that institutional investors have almost given up on extraordinary performance. Furthermore, the fiduciaries behind the institutions spend millions of dollars a year employing performance-measurement analysts with the primary incentive of protecting their fiduciary butts, and seemingly a secondary incentive to move money around from places that are about to perform better to places where they are about to quit performing well.

Certainly, in recent years the computer-based institutional activity of *program trading* has led the individual investor to question his own sophistication and ability to compete. Most of my friends in the securities industry dislike program trading because it leads to excessive volatility in the market, thereby disturbing individual investors and giving them the feeling that they are at a disadvantage to the institution. Somewhat secretly, I am in the opposite camp. In fighting for their eighths and quarters, if the institutions sent the market up and down 50% every month or so, my approach toward asset allocation should allow me to be a beneficiary and not a victim of their machinations. If some institution has managed to use computer program trading to perform outstandingly well, I have not as yet seen those results published.

A third category of investor concerns stems from an almost wavelike feeling that you as an investor *have to* or *should* invest in a momentarily fashionable and *profitable* investment vehicle. Many of these I put under the category of What Brokers Are Selling This Year. Years ago, when things were quiet in the securities business, you could put your feet up on the desk, relax, and recognize that the firm was not going to be very profitable for a while. In recent years, however, most major firms have hired creative geniuses to produce new *products* for their brokers to sell during quiet periods. You do not have to be very old to remember when it was very fashionable to trade options or buy option income funds. Further, I do not even have to have 10% of my money in Europe or 10% of my money in the Pacific Rim to sleep well. You could make a long list of what was *the thing to do* in any given year over the last decade. As a matter of fact, if I had done everything in my clients' portfolios that I either had to or should have done, there would be no room for a good common stock.

A fascinating aspect of the 1980s was how creative the investment community got in the fixed income section of a portfolio. Junk bonds, for example, were designed to attract buyers by offering a very high rate of current return, which, in most cases, proved to be too low a rate of current return considering the risks. Institutional investors bought most of these. At the moment, some of these institutions are using the standard American approach of suing the creators of the bonds for their losses instead of admitting that they violated their fiduciary duties to the funds they were managing when they bought the junk in the first place. If my cynicism is showing, let me quickly suggest that not all junk bonds were necessarily bad investments. Furthermore, at the other end of the fixed income spectrum, the investment community invented the zero-coupon bond, which as previously mentioned promised to pay the investor nothing (but appealed to many as the saver's approach to building an estate by totally forgoing the pleasures of income). You buy a zero-coupon bond at a substantial discount and it increases in value to its face amount at the time of maturity. In certain portfolios, zeros can be pretty good fixed income investments.

One of my major criticisms of almost all us investors (including institutions, many individuals, and even corporate management) is that our time horizons for investing are too short rather than too long. The members of the next generation are not the only ones who expect instant gratification. This human failing gets translated into a substantial number of our popular *products*. You buy a stock option, for example, on an excellent company, but your option frequently expires before the company can do for you in the short term what it could do for you over time.

The daily gyrations of the stock market itself have a tendency to keep us overly concerned with a short time frame. If you are among those who watch your stocks go up and down daily, if not more frequently, why not admit to yourself that you are wasting your time and simply check your stock prices every couple of weeks. Now, what do you do if you own a stock priced at $60 and some bad news comes out causing the stock to drop six points? Before you join the crowd selling the stock, simply ask yourself whether that particular event was really worth 10% of the value of your company. It is the emotional market reactions of this nature that give some credence to the old Wall Street saying, "Buy on bad news, and sell on good."

Short selling, usually a short-term trading mechanism, involves selling a stock that we do not own with the expectation of buying it back later at a lower price to produce our profit. This type of investing strategy is not the psychological norm for most of us Americans. When we think of making a profit, we think of buying something low and having it rocket upward. Certainly, there are people who are psychologically, as well as analytically, capable of being good short sellers. Personally, I am a natural optimist, so I do not engage in short selling. I tell myself that managements are hired by shareholders to improve companies, not make them worse, and it is the responsibility of the board of directors to do something about it if management is not solving the company's problems.

Occasionally, experts as well as vast numbers of the public seem to get hung up on certain types of securities. For example, as well known as they are, mutual funds, in my mind, are neither good nor bad investment vehicles in themselves. They can certainly be used, instead of individual securities, to attain the investing objectives of a great number of individual investors. The important consideration, of course, is to select the fund that fits what you are trying to do with the money and to choose the management that will do it for you. Probably worth mentioning in the context of investment policy is the fact that most mutual funds are well diversified, and this diversification has a moderating effect on the price movement of the fund. This leads me, on occasion, to rank a particular fund one group higher in our asset allocation model than I would each of the individual stocks within the fund. A very blue-chip stock fund, for example, even one laced liberally with high-grade growth stocks, could be regarded as a Group II investment because of the moderating effect on price movement by the diversification offered by the fund (the whole bunch of high-grade Group IIIs might equal a Group II holding).

The stock-option contracts previously mentioned are other examples of generic types of security that are not necessarily good nor bad investment vehicles in themselves. In this example, however, they are applicable only to a narrow number of qualified investors and generally, once again, for short periods of time. With stock options, historically, too many small investors assumed a great deal of short-term risk and paid the price for it.

The same kind of generic labeling is occasionally applied to *convertible securities*. Convertibles are bonds or preferred stocks that can be exchanged into common stock if the common appreciates in price enough to make the conversion attractive. Now, I do not know why you would buy a convertible bond just because it is convertible into common, especially in a company you do not like. Convertibles are simply hybrid securities that require a little mathematical exercise before you decide you would rather buy the convertible bond of an attractive company rather than the common stock or instead of just a bond. Do the mathematics, compare the yields, figure the premium, know precisely why you are buying the convertible bond instead of the common. It is all eighth-grade stuff, so I won't bore you with it. Just do it. In addition, watch out for call features if you pay a premium for the bond. An unexpected call can be a quick way to pay a high price for the common stock.

Do not worry about not knowing it all. You do not have to know it all. Furthermore, you as an individual can compete very successfully with *them*, the *big kids* of the investment world. Spend more time thinking about and improving your own capabilities and limitations, and spend no time worrying about the institutional investors. Our greatest fear is probably the fear of the unknown. Well, in the investment world, a lot of the unknown is not worth knowing. You might wish you were better at cyclical-stock selection, but you do not have to invest much in cyclical stocks to be successful in investing. Personally, I wish I were better at turnaround situations, but I can live without them. In fact, you might even get all the way through your life without ever understanding a gold-indexed *bear* bond or owning a Eurodollar future—certainly I will.

•

New Century—Slow Yourself Down...

I was delighted to find that the myths and fears I mentioned ten years ago are still myths and fears. We have a few new myths and probably a new fear that we deserve to have. The real new fear, if you want one of course, comes from the popularity of a historically high stock market. This certainly doesn't obliterate my conviction that you as an individual can compete very successfully with the big kids of the investment world.

One of the feelings I've had in reviewing my old thoughts is that American investors have compressed the amount of time dedicated to worthwhile activities like investing. In today's world, for example, the institutional investors, even more than individual investors, have adopted an almost cult-like preoccupation with short-term performance. Mutual fund managers know full well that their performance over such a lengthy period as three months will cause billions of dollars to move from one manager to another. Investing well is a process that requires years, not months, to bear fruit. As I said, people visit me today saying little more than "Make me rich, Hunter." Most of them will give me a few months or a year, but their idea is that "people out there" are getting rich today, and they would like to be among them by Tuesday. This is occurring at the same time that I am having more than normal difficulty (because of the high market) finding stocks to buy in which I have confidence. Even those who still believe we can become successful from forecasting the stock market would certainly not contend we can do so on a short-term basis. Oddly enough, my own time horizon, or time expectation, for a company to perform well is getting longer as I get older instead of shorter. Further, I find myself more pleased with a quiet stock that seems to have little risk at the time I buy it and ultimately turns out to have a very good performance. I've frequently made the comment that a good adviser and his client almost always have a bit of friction because the good adviser wants the client to do what should be done, and the client wants the adviser to do that which seems to be making people very wealthy at the moment.

CHAPTER 16

When You Get Rich

THE BEAUTY OF DEMOCRACY IS THAT IT PROVIDES FREEDOM to the individual. We have an obligation to ourselves to express this freedom in a unique and individual way, in both our opinions and our investments. One of the few joys of getting older is that we care less about what other people think of us and perhaps more about what they really think. I find myself not caring much anymore who somebody is (I can't remember their names anyway), but it seems more and more important whether I enjoy them, even in brief encounters, talking with them and exchanging ideas. I encourage you to express your point of view on most any subject. In my family, having a strong viewpoint with very little knowledge of the subject goes back at least a generation or two.

The pursuit of happiness is more important than the pursuit of wealth. I have known a few people for whom the correlation between the two is very strong and I feel a little sorry for them. This business of investing should be fun and to many people it isn't. I have known a few people who spend entirely too much time on it without being happy with the results. There is something to the theory of *benign neglect*, because I think many investors do better by not fussing too much with their stocks. If you own a good company, reading the quarterly reports in many cases is probably enough.

As I mentioned, investing is something like a complicated kid's game that you are allowed to keep playing when you grow up. My viewpoint is certainly not shared by everyone. Some people just hate spending time with their investments. Knowing your tolerance or enjoyment for time spent on your own investments is worthy, something like staying within your own limitations. Certainly, plenty of financial advisers/brokers are willing to help. Frankly, if I had to pick only one trait for a financial adviser, it wouldn't be brains; it would be empathy. I think a good adviser has a feeling for a client/friend and helps translate and implement this individual's investment policy.

The primary aim of this book is educational. If you happened to learn something, it would make me happy. I strongly believe that education is the only solution to our problems in an increasingly complex society. It is the only means of protecting our democratic and capitalistic privileges, which, in turn, allows us the opportunity to enjoy a good standard of living. Fortunately, we can always keep learning. Keeping informed is the only way to stay ahead and win in our society. Unfortunately, without the education to deal with this complex world, many people are unable to win. It certainly makes advising young people easy: Find something you enjoy (happiness) and become very good at it (education) in order to compete successfully and be a winner. The most difficult aspect of education for me is not to arrive at a conclusion but to appreciate the other person's perspective. You, particularly you young kids, are supposed to give me that. Oddly enough, I welcome your rejection of some of my ideas, so I submit them with the hope that you will challenge them, amend them, and improve them. It would be great fun for me to sit down with a half-dozen of you who have read this book and have you tell me where I am wrong.

Once you get rich, the question you must deal with becomes what to do with all the money. I have discovered only two good uses for money after we have paid the basic necessities of life (including cable TV, of course): Reinvest it or give it away. When you buy stock in good growing companies, you are contributing capital that, combined with the efforts of the employees, helps the company to grow and to provide the goods and services that, in turn, increase the standard of living of everyone who buys them. If the company's products or services are worthwhile, are cheaper or better, and the company makes a profit, continues to grow, and provides more jobs, then it is fulfilling my concept of social investing. We should learn the company's viewpoints on social policy questions, and the shareholders should approve of them or voice their objections. You should remember that by being an investor in a company with decent products or services, you are sponsoring something economically worthwhile. For me, the most fun of all is investing in a smaller company and watching it grow and succeed. I take the pledge that I will not become too conservative as I get older and stop investing in smaller companies. Too many successful businessmen do that much too early in their lives.

The second good use for excess money is to give it away. In this competitive, capitalistic society, some of us are fortunate enough to be winners, but, obviously, some are unfortunate enough to be losers. In today's world, the question is not whether or not we will take care of the unfortunate; it is whether it should be done in the public or the private sector. The public sector involves the federal, state, and local governments, through taxation, with competing interest groups attempting to administer aid to those who need it. I think most of you will agree with me, after you think about it for a bit, that we are much more efficient and effective in providing such aid in the private sector directly through individual volunteers without the red tape and enormously expensive bureaucratic government programs. In any event, the satisfaction you feel in achieving material success is small in comparison to the joy of being able to help others less financially able than yourself to win in our capitalistic world of opportunities. If we can give back both time and money to those less fortunate, we will be expressing our individualism, our freedom, our ideals, and maybe even take a step toward our pursuit of happiness.

College students must sacrifice none of their idealism to be successful in their careers or their investments. It is a myth to think otherwise. The most successful businessmen and investors I have known have had a very high degree of ethics and idealism. I am not saying that your high personal standards will not occasionally cost you money or cause you discomfort. They are almost bound to do so. Therefore, you will have troubles along the way. For what it's worth, the only two solutions I found that help when you're in trouble are to work harder and to help somebody else.

I am not sure that investing and making lots of money is all that important in the larger scheme of things. A few years ago I gave a one-hour-a-week course at an inner-city high school because I was feeling a little out of touch with the next generation. I seem to excel at getting good nonpaying jobs. One day, being unprepared, I asked them to do the work. I wanted them to define *success* and I put the key words on the blackboard. Very quickly, we had *money, power, position, fame,* etc., but then they began to mix in *happiness, good health, challenge,* and a few more different kinds of words. After half an hour or so, I suggested they look at all the words we had written and try to put them together in a pattern. What they then decided was that there are two kinds of success: an external success and an internal success. The external success included the words like *money* and *power,* and the internal success included words like *happiness* and a *feeling of well-being.* Finally, they decided that internal success was considerably more important than external success. I gave the whole class an A that day.

The End...

Index

Notes

Notes

_____

_____

_____

_____

_____

_____

_____

_____

_____

_____

_____

_____

_____

_____

_____

_____

_____

_____